PHONICS IN LEARNING TO READ

By ELLEN C. HENDERSON

Reading Can Be Fun

Phonics in Learning to Read

With TWILA L. HENDERSON

Learning to Read and Write

Phonics
in Learning
to Read

A Handbook for Teachers

by

ELLEN C. HENDERSON

An Exposition–University Book

EXPOSITION PRESS   NEW YORK

Dedicated to the teachers whose encouragement has resulted in this book, and chiefly to Jerrilyn C. Black, who did much of the research.

E. C. H.

EXPOSITION PRESS INC.

386 Park Avenue South   New York, N.Y. 10016

FIRST EDITION

EP 45712

CONTENTS

INTRODUCTION

Phonics in Learning to Read is a result of my having said to a woman who was examining my book for adults, *Learning to Read and Write*, published by Holt, Rinehart, and Winston, "In twenty-five years this book will seep down. Then no child will fail in his first learning-to-read experiences."

"Why wait?" I decided. "I can do something about it now."

Here is the book.

Its presentation of inner speech proves conclusively that the reader can "make out" the unknown word without having to be "told" what it is. He can hear an inner pronunciation of the word. If its meaning fits the context, he continues reading. If not, he seeks help.

In the English language the twenty-one consonant letters which represent the twenty-five consonant sounds are the framework of the words. When these consonants are pronounced correctly, the dozens of vowel values—spelled by only five letters—take their places naturally. This is possible because the vowel sounds are made into what they are by changes in the shape of the mouth cavity. The changes in shape are caused by the movements which occur while the tongue, lips, jaws, and soft palate are producing the consonant sounds.

Test this by observing what happens while *first* is being pronounced. For the sound of *f*, the upper teeth help to close the mouth cavity. The jaws have to open to permit the tongue to go to its positions for the *rst*. The vowel which emerges is the needed sound. In the word *remember,* three values of the vowel letter *e* are produced in the same "natural" way. The inner speech skeleton is r—m—mb—r.

The major difficulty in learning to read the English language is the alphabet.There are three alternatives for simplifying the difficulties:

1. Revise the alphabet.
2. Undergo spelling reform.
3. Find a way to succeed with the present alphabet.

The first two methods may someday become realities. Spelling is reforming itself, especially in popular advertising, and revisions of parts of the alphabet for the learning-to-read stage already are being used. However, these methods can have the drawbacks of inconsistent coding and the necessity for learners to shift from the new symbols to the regular alphabet in order to read the current print.

The method proposed in this book is the third alternative. It does not replace any of the necessary steps in the learning process. Instead, it presents ideas and a plan for use in teaching the early stages in the reading process.

This system, which is based upon the consonants and the combinations that are consistent enough to offer reliable guides to beginning readers, is fully explained in the book. This workable and practical method has been used successfully with young children, teen-agers, and non-reading adults in beginning as well as in "remedial" reading.

PHONICS IN LEARNING TO READ

CHAPTER I

Why Consonants Rather Than Vowels Are Useful in Learning to Read

The reader is asked to consider for a moment the following paired words.

yodel	model	eight	sleight	through	thorough
pare	are	have	gave	tough	trough
flood	brood	near	pear	robe	adobe
page	damage	on	son	wind	wind (blow)
here	there	low	how	sewer	sewer (sew)
were	where	but	put	gone	done
boot	foot	treat	create	done	lone
few	sew	safe	café	above	rove

These pairs of words illustrate the problem confronting the reader. In each pair are the same vowel letters but they are pronounced in a different way. The consonant letters are pronounced in the same way regardless of the vowel sounds or letters.

The alphabet, an imperfect code

The alphabet is a code system in which the letters have been assigned the language sounds. Learning to read—and spell —would be less difficult if each letter represented one particular sound. If this were the case, whenever a particular letter was used no other written symbol would represent that sound.

This requirement is met in the coding of quantities and arithmetic signs. The number 8 means only the quantity eight, not five or seven or nine, and no other number means eight. The plus sign always means to add, and not occasionally to divide or subtract. When addition is called for, the sign for subtraction or division is not used.

Reliability of alphabet letters

Obviously the alphabet does not meet the requirements for perfect coding. Although eight of the letters (*b, k, l, m, q, r, v* and *w*) never represent any sound other than their own, four of the eight are silent in some words (*thumb, know, walk, answer*). Each of six letters (*d, f, j, n, p,* and *z*) carries one sound besides its own: *d* is *t* only with *ed* (*looked*), *f* is *v* in only one word (*of*), *j* is *j* except in "foreign" words (*San Juan, José*), *n* helps spell the *ng* sound (*sing, ink, finger*), *p* with *h* is *f* (*phrase*), and *z* rarely is *s*.

Note that the remaining seven consonants (*c, g, h, s, t, x,* and *y*) are used to represent or help to represent twelve consonant sounds. Five of the twelve sounds (*g, h, s, t, y*) are spelled by single letters. The seven others (*ng, ch, sh, th, th, wh, zh*) are spelled by two letters. However, in many words the *ng* sound is represented by the *n* (*finger, ink*) and in all words either *s* or *z* represents the *zh* sound (*measure, azure*). The five vowel letters (*a, e, i, o, u*) are used to represent the fifteen definite vowel sounds, the four diphthongs, the neutral vowel, and the numerous gradations of vowel values with which the words of the language are so plentifully supplied. For perfect coding, the alphabet would need twenty-five symbols for the consonants plus four for the definite diphthongs and many times fifteen for the variations of the vowels.

The problems are multiplied because sounds which have been assigned to some of the letters have also been assigned to others.

Reliability of vowel letters

The *a*: The letter *a* uses nine different sounds in words (*ate, fair, at, ask, father, walk, cause, onward,* and *alone*).

In *faux pas*, the *a* uses the sound of *o* that is in *go*.

In *father*, the *a* uses the sound of *o* that is in *on*.

The *a* in the last syllable of *package* is the sound of *i* that is in *it*.

The sound of the *a* in *care* is the same as the vowel sound in *their*.

In the last syllable of *meringue*, the *i* uses the sound of *a* in *at*.

The vowel sound in *ought* is spelled with *a* in *daughter*.

The *a* in *many* uses the sound of *e* that is in *then*.

To compound the confusion, the letter *a* is not the only letter representing the vowel sound in *late*. Other words present this sound by the use of different letters and combinations, such as—

play	neighbor	ballet	break	Beethoven
they	campaign	maid	Fae	toupee

Yet the same letters, pronounced as the *a* that is in *ate*, are pronounced differently in other words. Notice these pairs:

neighbor	height	toupee	carefree	ballet	wallet
Beethoven	beetle	they	key	vein	receive
break	breath	play	ay	campaign	pair
maid	plaid	aisle	air	maid	said

In addition, the sounds of the letter *a* may change two or three times within the same word.

adamant	canary	drama	patriarch
adoration	cannonade	fallacy	plantation
animal	cantaloupe	favorable	saturate
baggage	cantata	fantasia	vagrant
ballad	carriage	harass	valiant
Canada	character	Indiana	valedictorian
Canadian	cravat	macadam	Wasatch

The letter *e*: The vowel sound in the word *me* is written in different ways.

| see | believe | amoeba | machine |
| sea | receive | people | key |

The vowel sound in the word *went* is written differently.

| went | said | breath | friend |
| many | says | leopard | heifer |

The letter *i*: The diphthong sound in *ice* is written in various ways.

ride	height	try	eye	guide
island	pie	by	I	geyser
aisle	high	buy	cycle	light

The vowel sound in *it* is written in many ways.

it	build	baby	minute
women	sieve	sincerely	message
England	sympathy	lovely	college

The letter *o*: The vowel sound in the word *go* is written in many ways with many letters and combinations.

| go | bowl | though | hoe | plateau |
| road | sew | bouquet | yeoman | chauffeur |

The vowel sound in *on* is written in many ways.

| on | are | thought | encore | memoir |
| song | father | auction | sergeant | awning |

The vowel sound in *room* uses different letters.

room	true	group	shoe	to
rule	lieu	buoy	blew	too
fruit	neutral	beautiful	through	two

The vowel sound in *look* is written differently.

| sure | put | soot | should | Ruhr |

The letter *o* is used differently in spelling these words:

go	snow	two	son	one
road	how	to	lemon	Ouija
oasis	shoulder	food	word	look
people	bough	flood	journal	should
hoe	enough	floor	colonel	for
shoe	thought	buoy	oil	corn
does	through	woman	boy	core
wore	thorough	women	buoyant	memoirs

The letter *u*: The diphthong *u* is written in different ways.

use	few	imbue	feud	you

The vowel sound in *up* is written with different letters.

sun	one	does	young
son	once	flood	enough

The other diphthongs: The diphthong in *out* is spelled with *ow* in many words.

out	how

The diphthong in *oil* is spelled with *oy* and *uo*.

oil	boy	buoyant

Further inconsistencies

Letters representing the vowels in any given word have alternate pronunciations in other words. In turn, these letters representing alternate pronunciations represent sounds spelled by still different letters. For example, the *ou* of *youth* is pronounced differently in *young*, and the vowel sound in *young* is spelled differently in *up*. Note that it is the vowel letters which show inconsistencies.

youth	young	young	up
lone	done	done	fun
done	lone	lone	though
put	use	use	few
blew	sew	sew	go
aisle	plaid	plaid	bad
bad	father	father	on
rough	though	though	snow
grow	how	how	bough
through	though	though	hoe
yeoman	people	people	meet
depot	pot	pot	fought
brood	blood	blood	son
chief	cried	cried	aisle
through	thought	thought	haunt
numeral	number	number	once
shoulder	should	should	wood
journal	our	our	flower

The letters of the dipthong *ou-ow* are used to spell other sounds.

how	snow		
out	rough	thought	through
youth	could	shoulder	journal

Vowel rules are unreliable

In attempts to make the unreliable vowels have some semblance of reliability, various rules have been devised to guide a reader. Nevertheless, formulation and application of rules seem almost pointless because of numerous inconsistencies. Some of the exceptions to common vowel rules will point up the inconsistencies which complicate the problem of reading when the vowels are used as keys.

One rule: When only one vowel is in a word or syllable, the pronunciation is usually "short."

Large families of words, of course, adhere to this rule.

ant	it	not	run	Ralph	rust
back	lamp	of	snip	patch	snatch
can	let	off	slip	which	scotch
fleck	link	rock	shock	dish	ditch
held	mad	rug	top	much	bend

How, then, are such words as the following to be read?

I	a	the	be	to	two	so	ski

A further rule is obviously necessary to exclude the above exceptions: if only one vowel is in a word or syllable, and if it is followed by a consonant, it is usually "short." *

Yet there are numerous exceptions to the rule to exclude those exceptions. Many words are not pronounced with a "short" vowel even though they meet the requirements of such a rule.

bar	worn	watch	lawn	ton	sew
sir	bind	blind	show	most	her
old	light	watt	few	cart	fur
surf	sign	put	now	wash	worm

In addition, because of such words as *play, plow, snow, blew, key, draw,* and *boy,* rules covering still other exceptions must be formulated. Yet inconsistencies continue to appear. Why, for example, is the letter *e* in *sew* and *few* pronounced with different vowel sounds? And why the different pronunciation of the *o* in *plow* and *show*?

Furthermore, exceptions to the rule requiring the "short" sound of a single vowel to be followed by a consonant are found in words of more than one syllable. The fact is that only accented syllables tend to have a "long" or a "short" vowel sound. The word *animal* is an example. The last two syllables do not

---

* In this book the words *short* and *long* are printed "short" and "long" to avoid misuse of the terms. Phonetically, the *a* in *ask* is as short as the *a* in *at,* and the *oo* in *room* is as long as the *o* in *old.*

have full-value vowel sounds. Rather, the vowels are pronounced as neutrals with only the accented vowel being "short"—*an—m—l*.

A *second rule:* When a one-syllable word ends in *e* preceded by a consonant which in turn is preceded by a vowel, the final *e* generally is silent and the vowel before the consonant is "long."

Many words follow this rule but many do not, as the examples show.

alive—live	fuse—rude	change—charge
lone—one	made—bade	gave—have
stove—love	mere—were	home—come
wove—move	lone—gone	bare—are

Similar confusions may appear when a learner is confronted with words of more than one syllable.

drive—native	rice—notice	service—office
dance—attendance	cage—cabbage	garage
lace—populace	dine—medicine	machine

A *third rule:* When two vowels come together, the first one is usually "long" and the second is usually silent.

Many words conform to the rule. These and numerous words with *ea* do:

rain	read	receive	tried	boat	hue

However, many words do not conform.

pair	learn	chief	broad	build	youth
laugh	steak	pier	boil	guile	young
squash	tear	carries	poem	fruit	would
	dread	diet		guard	ghoul
	beau			buoyant	journal
	weight			buoy	bough
	neutral			duel	enough
	create			duet	thought
	area				

The combination *ea* may be pronounced at least nine ways, only one of which conforms to the rule.

(can) read	learn	heart
(had) read	break	react
(did) tear	sergeant	realize

Consonants as reliable guides

Neither the vowels nor the rules relating to them serve as reliable guides to the beginning reader. However, such guides are found among the consonants.

Although some consonants are as inadequately coded as are the vowels, some of them approach the criteria for perfect coding, and others have limited variations which are consistent enough to be helpful.

It is because of the reliable consonants that any individual has learned to read, regardless of what phonics system he thinks he learned.

In fact, what has long been called "vowel" phonics in theory has been "consonant" phonics in practice.

A new look at an old method

Teachers and writers of phonics materials have been using consonants as keys to reading even though they may have thought they were teaching "vowels." They may have been doing this without fully realizing the implications of what they actually were doing. Examination of almost any "system" of phonics that is concerned with early vowel experience will furnish evidence of this unknowing use of consonants rather than vowels.

Frequently an early drill, thought to treat vowels, will instead deal with "word families." The list below illustrates words with several "families."

will	sit	dig	hat	cap	had
mill	hit	big	rat	nap	sad
fill	pit	fig	bat	tap	lad
kill	quit	jig	vat	yap	glad

When a beginner is taught to "read" these families, he is told the sound of the vowel and the final consonant. Then he is asked to figure out what the words are. Notice that he is not asked to figure out the vowel and the family ending; the vowel sound, common to all words of the list, has been supplied beforehand.

In word-family lists, the vowels and some of the consonants are held constant throughout the list. The beginner, knowing the sound of the ending, is relieved of figuring out these sounds and thus can concentrate his attention on the initial consonants. In other words, when the difficult vowel is standardized, he can bypass vowel difficulties while he copes with the consonants. After he has learned the consonants, he is then able to cope with the vowels. He must, however, read the initial consonants.

To further point up the fact that consonant-style rather than vowel-style phonics is being employed by such a system, consider what a list would look like if vowels were actually being studied as claimed.

Dan	Dane	Don	Dean
dun	dine	den	down
din	done	din	deign

If vowel phonics were really being used, the student would be told the sound of the consonant which is the same in each word, as in the above. He would therefore not need to "read" the consonants in each word, but would need to study the vowels.

The above lists, of course, are not the type commonly found in phonics books or on chalkboards. It would, in fact, be unfortunate to have such a list. Correct reading of such words requires the application of several vowel rules, an unnecessarily complex process for beginners in comparison with the word-family approach. Furthermore, some of the vowel rules break down completely in the simple lists given above; *done* does not have the "long" sound of *o*, and *deign* is not pronounced as *dean*.

If a teacher uses word families in order to get the learner to recognize the word-family ending the next time he sees it, he is teaching the family by word-recognition or sight-teaching techniques rather than by vowel phonics.

If the learner does recognize the word-family ending the next time he sees it, and is then able to figure out the initial consonant, he has read a word through a combination of previous sight learning and consonant phonics.

Further evidence of failure by teachers to recognize that they are teaching by consonants is found in the common listing together of words which one vowel rule ("A word ending with the letter *e* preceded by a vowel and a consonant has the vowel 'long' with the final *e* silent") does not cover. Such lists contain not only such words as *June, use,* and *cute,* which follow the rule, but also *rude, Luke,* and *flute,* which do not follow the rule.

Another evidence of the unknowing use of consonant phonics before vowels is found in a series of words spelled with the same vowel letters.

broom	shook	good	poor
brook	school	flood	school
floor	flood	soot	wool
flood	brook	root	took

The student is asked to read each word by trying out three possible sounds of *oo* until he finds a word he has in his vocabulary. Such a procedure is, of course, a sound one; it is one of the basic techniques by which readers separate words they know from words they do not recognize. Missing, however, by the user of such a group of words, is the realization that such a trying-out process FOLLOWS the learning of the consonants. The reader tries out the possible sounds of the vowel until he finds a sound which fits with the consonants to make a word he recognizes.

The "vowel" system does not work. If it has worked, why do we have reading improvement (remedial) classes for teaching what might have been learned at the beginning?

The neutral vowel

In the spelling of every word in the English language there is at least one vowel. In all words except two (*I* and *a*) there is at least one consonant, although two other words (*oh* and *you*) might with consistency be spelled by *o* and *u*.

In words with two or more syllables, one syllable will be accented. Words with more than three syllables may have a secondary accent, which in dictionaries may be marked in lighter ink than the primary accent.

During ordinary speech the vowels in most unaccented syllables lose their particular characteristics. Instead, they carry a transition sound. This transition sound is voiced but does not have a characteristic tongue movement. It is simply the sound of the voice as the tongue, the lips, the jaws, and the soft palate move from forming one consonant to forming another.

Each full-value vowel has its characteristic tongue position or positions inside the mouth cavity. In pronouncing the vowel in the word *me*, for example, the middle of the tongue is lifted toward the soft palate. In the vowel sound in *pin*, the tongue is slightly lower. In *went* the tongue moves a small degree lower. In *want* the back of the tongue is noticeably lower.

For one-syllable words, the tongue forms the necessary and particular sound required for each sounded vowel. Each word carries an accent, for there is no other syllable present. There is no neutral vowel in such words.

Pronounce the following short words, noting how the tongue assumes a definite and different tongue position for each of the sounded vowels.

late	meet	pin	room
hat	best	own	book
old	gone	sun	word

Do the same with the four diphthongs.

bite	Butte	boil	bow
bind	Buhl	boy	bound

In contrast, however, are words of more than one syllable. Only one of the syllables will be definitely accented. The other syllables tend to have unaccented vowels with the vowel merely a voiced transition between consonants. For example, to say the word *divide*, we give to the letter *i* in the first syllable a sound much like that in the first syllable of *alone*. We say d—*vide*, accenting the second syllable.

The unaccented sound is the neutral vowel.

Note how the pronunciation of the vowel letter changes according to its position in an accented or an unaccented syllable in words like these:

macadam	cantata	division	remember
potato	honor	extravagant	celebrate
Alabama	Canada	undulate	skeleton

The neutral vowel in sentences

In connected speech, words, like syllables, tend to lose their accented vowels. For example, the words below when spoken individually have thirteen syllables, with nine accented vowels and only four vowels that are unaccented.

morning	am	to
going	I	in
exhibit	the	the

But when the thirteen syllables are spoken in a thought context, there are ten unaccented and only three accented.

Written: I am going to the exhibit in the morning.
Spoken: I -m g--ng t- th- -xhib-t -n th- morn-ng.

As a matter of fact, if the sentence were spoken in an emotional manner, making the time of going exactly and specifi-
cally clear, the entire sentence might be spoken with only one
clear, full-value vowel sound.

Written: I am going to the exhibit in the morning.
Spoken: I —m g———ng t— th— —xh—b—t —n th— morn—ng.

Consonants remain stable

At first thought it may seem logical that neutralization similar to that of the vowels should be present in the pronunciation
of consonants.

Such is not the case. The consonant sounds remain stable.
In all words and in all word positions a given consonant is produced by the same adjustments. In fact, any slight deviation
from the characteristic tongue movement produces a sound
which is not only definitely inaccurate but also entirely different.
For example, when the tongue fails to make the movement
needed for the sound of n in *I don't know*, something like *I dod
dow* or *I dot tow* is heard.

To further illustrate the fact that a consonant is not modified by accent or by the sounds which may precede or follow
it (as vowels are), consider the word *divided* or the word
momentum. Each of these words presents a consonant in the
initial, the medial, and the final word position. The tongue makes
the same movement for each of the three *d*'s and the three *m*'s
are made exactly alike.

Differences in any given consonant as it occurs in words
show up in amount of time producing it rather than in the sound
itself. For example, in *did not* four movements of the tongue are
required to produce the two *d*'s, the *n*, and the *t* (*d—d n—t*).

When the *did not* becomes *didn't* and the time is thus reduced, the tongue still makes the four characteristic movements.

Use of stable or reliable consonants allows learners to by-pass the difficulties of the vowels and the unstable consonants.

Methods and order of teaching the consonants are presented in other chapters. Here, however, the consonants are examined according to their reliability.

Nine of the twenty-one consonant letters are effectively coded in that the reader can instantly use the sound—or its absence when it is silent—in word recognition. Five are reasonably well coded in that they use their alphabet sound except in just one definite word position. Five of the other seven are reliable in definite word positions.

Nine well-coded consonant letters

The *m:* The letter *m* carries no sound other than its own; furthermore, it is the only letter which carries this sound. A reader encountering this letter in any position in any word may use it in word recognition. Though the letter *m* is silent in some technical words (mneumonics), the early reader will neither see such words nor have them in his vocabulary.

Note the reliability of this letter regardless of its position at the beginning, middle, or ending of a word when blended with other words.

Initial	Medial	Final	Blends
milk	summer	from	smile
must	coming	come	company
man	animal	them	chipmunk
moon	family	game	arm
Monday	moment	room	elm

The *r:* The letter *r* carries no sound other than its own and is the only letter which carries this sound. A reader may use the *r* in word recognition every time he sees it. Note how the *r* carries its sound in all positions and in all blends.

Initial	Medial	Final	Blends
rain	around	here	break
ripe	very	dear	horse
rose	carry	bear	fried
rapid	fury	river	country
rodeo	tomorrow	roller	spring
racket	carol	care	string

The *v:* The *v* carries no other sound than its own. Thus the reader may be taught that in all positions and in all words the letter *v* carries the sound of *v*.

Initial	Medial	Final	Blends
very	divide	give	velvet
visit	lovely	have	svelt
village	diving	save	valve
vote	evening	live	harvest
vine	river	love	twelve
vowel	seven	five	servant

The *b:* The letter *b* is the only carrier of the sound of *b,* and it does not have any other sound assigned to it. Occasionally, however, it is silent. It is silent in words like *thumb* and *subtle.* In such words the *b* sound is so difficult to articulate that inner speech ignores it.

Note the reliability of this letter regardless of its location in words or when blended with other consonants.

Initial	Medial	Final	Blends
big	cabin	rob	black
boy	robber	cab	brown
boat	cabbage	scrub	November
book	cubical	cube	subtract
bench	rubbed	rub	blackbird

The *l:* The letter *l* carries no sound other than the *l* and it is the only carrier of the sound of *l.* When the sound is difficult to pronounce, the *l* may be silent (*walk, chalk*). Careful speakers sound the *l* in similar words (*milk, silk*). When two *l*'s double up, the tongue usually makes a double movement (*smaller, falling*) but not so at the beginning or the end of words (*small, fall, Lloyd*).

Note the reliability of this letter in all words and blends.

Initial	Medial	Final	Blends
like	yellow	all	world
leaf	belong	tell	sparkle
live	sailing	sail	glass
loud	illiterate	little	play
last	relay	small	always
lunch	stealing	until	flower
little	milk	while	children

The *k:* The *k* carries no sound other than its own, and when it is silent (*knee, know, knight*) inner speech seems to find it too difficult to bother with.

Note how the letter *k* carries the same sound in all word positions and in blends.

Initial	Medial	Final	Blends
keen	cooky	cook	Ku Klux Klan
kind	walking	walk	handkerchief
king	basket	book	asks
key	cracker	thank	work
kettle	taking	desk	breakfast
kitten	crooked	crook	milk

The *q:* The letter *q* always represents the sound of *k* and is always followed by the letter *u.* In some words (*antique, bouquet, croquet*) the *u* is silent. In many words (*quiet, quickly, squirrel*) the *u* carries the sound of *w.*

Initial	Medial	Final	Blends
quiet	require	antique	inquest
question	bouquet	critique	Albuquerque
quart	request	opaque	square
queue	coquette		exquisite
quick	croquet		squash

The *w:* The *w* (when not teamed with *h* to make *wh*) is a reliable letter if a rather minor restriction is kept in mind. In some foreign words the *w* is pronouunced as a *v* (*Wagner*). In general, such words may be disregarded in early reading because they are not likely to be encountered by the beginner nor to be in his vocabulary.

Occasionally, the *w* is silent (*saw, know, knowledge, drawn*). In such words the *w* is not easily spoken. However, the sound of *w* is easily produced after the sound of *h* in words that are spelled *wh* (*where, white, why*). (Such words are sounded *hwere, hwite, hwy.*)

Note that the letter *w* carries its own sound in different positions in words and in blends.

Initial	Medial	Final	Blends
were	away	sow	twelve
with	following	sew	always
went	tower	grow	backward
wish	flower	how	inward
water	awake	plow	dwarf
would	northward	now	swing
warm	awash	show	otherwise

The *z:* The letter *z* carries only the sound of *z* in so many words that beginners can be taught to produce the *z* sound whenever it is encountered. Words in which the *z* is not pronounced as a *z* sound fall into two classifications: such words (*mezzo, zwieback*) as are not in a beginner's vocabulary, and

some other words (*waltz, pretzel, Fitzgerald*) that are pronounced with the sound of *s* because the sound of *z* is not
easily pronounced immediately after the sound of *t*. The more
easily pronounced *s* sound will be substituted automatically by
inner speech. In many words, like *azure* and *seizure*, the sound
of *zh* is pronounced, but the *zh* sound is begun with a *z* sound
even in words with the letter *s* (*measure, pleasure*); so that
when the eyes focus on the letter *z*, the reader can use the *z*
in word recognition.

Note how the *z* letter carries the *z* sound in different positions in words. Note also that the *z* does not blend easily with
consonants.

Initial	*Medial*	*Final*	*Blends*
zero	trapezoid	buzz	Tzar
zoo	blizzard	blaze	
zebra	dozen	trapeze	
zeal	hazy	seize	
zipper	buzzard	breeze	

Consonants that have only two sounds

Five of the consonants have limited variations which are
consistent enough to be helpful. Until such time as the reader's
inner speech is well developed, he has to make a choice between
two sounds. If the first choice does not result in a word that fits
into the meaning of the sentence or the phrase, the reader can
try the second sound.

The five letters are *d, f, n, p,* and *j*. The first four never
carry more than the two sounds; but the *j* in some foreign words
may be another sound (*San José, San Juan*).

The *d*: The *d* is the only letter carrying the sound of *d*; and
the only time it carries any other sound is when the word has *ed*
at the end (*laughed, looked*). The *t* substitution occurs in words
of one syllable with only a few exceptions (*telegraphed, photo-*

graphed). The reason for the substitution seems to be that the sound of *t* is more easily made than the sound of *d*.

Notice the difference between these pairs of words:

smiled	laughed	buzzed	raced	shoved	pranced
moved	stopped	robbed	dropped	begged	walked
probed	looked	robed	dressed	changed	wrenched
eased	rushed	breathed	thanked	swathed	threshed

The second word of each pair uses the sound of *d* when it is spoken in two syllables, as any of them may be used in poetical writing. Most compound words ending in *ed* use the sound of *i* in *it*, instead of the sound of *e* in *end* as in these words:

| hunted | harvested | hounded | painted | gilded |
| wanted | hurried | carried | fainted | sorted |

A rule might be formulated about the connection between the voiced and unvoiced *d* and the way the final *d* is pronounced. But the rule would be of questionable value unless there were no exceptions. To offer a rule which has exceptions is like saying to a visitor, "Here is a chair but don't sit on it."

Fortunately, no rule is needed for words ending in *ed*. Inner speech follows the rule of talk and ignores the specific difficulty while taking the easy path, the spoken word.

Note how the letter *d* carries the alphabet sound in all word positions and in all blends.

Initial	*Medial*	*Final*	*Blends*
dwarf	handy	hand	handkerchief
dress	ready	read	goldfish
dark	hiding	hide	changed
desk	wordy	word	bird
dirty	golden	gold	dwindle
door	children	child	children
down	hundred	red	hundred

The *f*: The *f* is a fairly reliable letter. It carries only its own sound except in the word *of*. If this word is learned by sight, learners may know that at all other times the letter is sounded *f*.

Note how the letter carries its sound in different word positions and blends with other consonants.

Initial	Medial	Final	Blends
fast	careful	half	flag
field	selfish	leaf	frost
fleet	before	life	breakfast
friend	awful	off	shelf
first	refine	wolf	softly
fly	defend	if	wonderful

The *j*: The letter *j* is always in the initial or the medial position in words. It carries the sound heard in the name of the letter except in some words of foreign origin (*San Juan, San José, junta, Navajo*). Most of such words are proper names and, but for a fad—temporary or permanent—would begin with a capital letter.

Note that the *j* carries the same sound in all word positions and blends.

Initial	Medial	Blends
just	rejoice	object
jacket	reject	subject
jelly	project	adjective
jet	rejoin	adjacent

The *n*: The *n* is the only letter carrying the *n* sound. Beginners may be taught that the *n* uses the sound of *n* at the beginning and at the end of all words, but that within a word it may either represent the sound of *ng* (*ink, thank*) or help to spell the *ng* sound (*thing, sing*).

The *n* is silent in a few words (*hymn, column*). Little attention need be given to the silent *n* of the words which end with *mn*. Because we do not pronounce the *n* in talk, inner speech ignores it in reading.

Initial	Medial	Final	Blends
name	candy	nineteen	until
nasal	many	can	learner
near	window	seven	ninth
never	running	town	lend
note	enough	own	grand
noise		burn	ignore

The *p*: The letter *p* is the only carrier of the sound of *p*. It has its alphabet sound except when it is followed by *h* to spell the sound of the *f* (*telephone, phrase*) and when it is silent (*pneumonia, psalms*).

Note that the *p*—without the *h*—carries the same sound in all word positions and blends.

Initial	Medial	Final	Blends
part	depend	shop	pray
place	people	drape	spring
please	property	jump	shrimp
peace	happy	help	help
pump	purple	crop	napkin
pray	napkin	nap	purple

Consonants that have more than two sounds

After subtracting the nine consonants which the reader can use in words because of their nearly perfect reliability and the five which require the reader to choose between only two sound-possibilities, we have seven left to examine. The seven are *c, g, h, s, t, x,* and *y*.

The *c*: The letter *c* carries the sound of *s* in its alphabet name and in many words. It carries the sound of *k* in thousands of words. It uses the sound of *ch* in *cello* and *sh* in *concerto*. It has no sound of its own. Its only distinctive use is in helping to spell the two-letter *ch* sound. Yet this distinctive sound is

end of words it may be used to spell one o
he vowel letter *i* (*try, trying, lovely*). Within a
rup) it may be used to represent the vowel s
elled by all of the vowel letters and *y* (*myrtle,*
her, earn). The initial *y* usually is pronounced
a few words it is silent (*yule, playmate*).
der cannot be sure about the *y* at the end of w
y be silent. Whether it is pronounced will de
sition in a phrase. If it is in a position of emph
ounded. Note what happens in these phrases:

ord   they are not   the way to go

at the *y* is pronounced in all positions in these wo

Medial	*Final*	*Blends*	*Other Sou*
canyon	gray	canyon	try
beyond	they	barnyard	trying
lawyer	way	wayward	happy
barnyard	play	lawyer	carry

At first glance the letter *h* may seem to be the m
d letter of the alphabet because it is used in
six other sounds (*ch, ph, sh, th, th,* and *wh* as th
in, phone, she, this, thick, and *when*). Although
its own sound at the beginning of words (*ha*
tial *h* is silent in some words (*honest, honor*). Wi
may be silent (*rhyme, rhinoceros, neighbor, lig*
t). The *h* with *g* in *enough* uses the sound of
is either silent or helping to spell other sounds
(*school, chagrin*).
inal position, the *h* is so nearly silent that it is t
of breath (*oh, ah*).
tely, inner speech seems able to ignore silent *g* an
ertain about it, the automatic sound response shoul
d to words containing the silent *g*'s and *gh*'s whil
are learning words by "sight."

marred because the *ch* uses a *k* or *sh* sound in many words (*chorus, choir, chagrin, Chicago*). It is silent in some words (*science, scent*). In all consonant blends with *l* and *r* the *c* always carries the sound of *k* (*class, cream*).

For reading and spelling, some other letter—or no letter— would serve better.

The *c* appears in such guises as these:

As k	*As s*	*As sh*	*As ch*	*Silent*
can	cents	chagrin	church	science
picnic	circus	Chicago	chin	rock
scald	receive	musician	cello	
scrub	sentence	politician		
chorus				
picture				

Both reading and spelling would be much simplified if other letters were used instead of the *c*, and if all silent letters were omitted. If this were done, the words above would be printed:

kan	sents	shagrin	church	siens
piknik	sirkus	Shukago	chin	rok
skald	reseeve	muzishen	chello	
skrub	sentunse	politishen		
korus				
pikcher				

The *g*: The letter *g* is much overloaded. Its alphabet name adds a second sound, that of the *j* (*gem*). It helps to spell the *ng* sound (*singing*). It is silent in some words (*sign, gnat*). It is teamed with *h* in words in which both letters are silent (*night, thought*) and in words in which only the *h* is silent (*ghost, ghoul*). In some words (*laugh, enough*) the *gh* is sounded as the *f*.

In consonant blends with *l* and *r*, the *g* always carries the sound of *g* in *go* (*glad, grow*). It carries the same sound in all blends unless the sound of *j* is spoken more easily.

Beginners who can point to and name the alphabet lette[r] have developed the automatic sound response to the *j* sound ([*g*] in *gee*). Thus, although they can name the letter *g*, they shoul[d] learn words beginning with the sound *g* in *go* before they ar[e] taught words beginning with the *j* sound.

The words given here use both sounds.

Initial	Medial	Final	Blends
glad	wagon	wag	aglow
go	begin	beg	agree
green	beggar	brag	ground
gem	wager	wage	budge
gentle	paging	ridge	judge
gene	agenda	badge	wedge

The *s:* The letter *s* is much overworked. At the beginning of many words it carries its alphabet sound (*see, such*) but it also is sounded *sh* (*sure, sugar*). At the end the sound may be the *s* or the *z*, whichever sound is the more easily articulated. At any location within a word, the sound may be *s* or *z* or *sh* o[r] *zh* (*master, season, pressure, pleasure*). If *s* is followed by *c*[,] the *sc* may be a consonant blend (*scald, scamp*) or it may merely be the *s* sound with a silent *c* (*science, scent*).

The *s* is reliable, however, in all consonant blends except the *sc*. Note the sound of *s* in the following blends:

lobster	tense	scream	spring
subscribe	naps	skip	squirrel
bedstead	turnspit	slow	step
offset	turnstile	small	wistful
cliffs	horse	snow	string
rocks	first	spell	svelte
also	bursts	splinter	swing

The reader is greatly helped by the reliable *s*-blends. How-ever, he has to know about the multiple uses illustrated here[.]

s as s	s as z
sell	reason
sister	choose
lobster	busy
books	advisor
its	words

The *t:* The letter *t* is over[worked. It carries its alphabet] sound at the beginning of words[...] of the two-letter sounds (*this, t*[...]) which do not have an *e* before [...] words when the *t* is followed by [...] may be *ch* or *sh* (*picture, sectio*[n]) is sounded unless pronunciation i[s...]

Initial	Medial	Final
table	potato	want
time	wanted	hit
town	waited	met
tear	little	weight
tell	butter	night
tarnish	leftover	write
television	attract	rite

The *x:* The *x* has no sound o[f its own. Like] the *q*—uses sounds of other lette[rs... It is] sounded *ks, gz, z,* or *sh* (*six, exit,* [...]) free rides the *x* has.

x as ks	x as gz	x as z
six	exit	xylopho[ne]
x-ray	exist	anxiety
fix	exam	xylem
annex	auxiliary	Xerox

The *y:* The *y* poses a real pro[blem...]

toward th[e...] sounds of [...] (*myrtle,* [...]) which is [...] *word, firs*[t...] *yellow*).

The [...] Final *y* [...] upon its [...] it may b[e...]

say th[e...]

Not[e...]

Initia[l...]

you
youn[g]
yeste[rday]
youn[ger]

Th[e...] poorly [...] spelling [...] occur i[n...] carries [...] *hat*), t[...] in wor[ds...] and *th*[...] Moreo[ver...] many [...]

In [...] merest [...]

F[...] *gh*. To [...] be de[...] the le[...]

Initial	Medial	Final	Blends
have	perhaps	oh	perhaps
half	Idaho	ah	overhang
heard	behave	sigh	uphold
hurt	unhappy	high	inhabit
hush	household		inherit
hang	ahead		uphill

Two-letter consonant sounds

Many difficulties in learning to read spring from inadequate coding of seven consonant sounds existing in the language but not in the letters of the alphabet. Consequently, two adjustments occur in written language. The first is that sounds are assigned to letters which already carry a sound. The second is that they are assigned to a combination of two letters. (The seven are *ch, sh, th, th, zh* and *ng*).

For example, the letter *s* not only has to carry the *s* and the *z* sounds represented by the alphabet letters, but also the *sh* and *zh* sounds (*sure, Asia*). But the *zh* sound in *Asia* is represented by *s* (*measure*), and by *g* (*garage*). The *sh* (*shall*) is also represented by *c* (*concerto*), by *t* (*nation*), by *ch* (*Chicago, chivalry*), and by *s* (*sure*).

Other examples are: the letter *t*, which not only carries its alphabet sound but also the sound of *ch* (*nature*) and *sh* (*notion*), and the *ch* (*church*), which is also carried by *c* (*cello*) and by *t* (*picture, fixture*), and which carries two other sounds (*character, Chicago*).

This tangle might have been avoided at the time when letters were first assigned to the language sounds. The sounds now represented by the two-letter combinations *sh* and *ch* might consistently have been assigned to two of the three letters (*c, q, x*) that now carry sounds which other letters represent.

Fortunately, in the seemingly confused tangle of letters and sounds, enough pattern is present to allow a systematic approach to at least some of these sounds which have no alphabet letter.

The *wh* sound: The *wh* poses a problem because the *h* is sounded before the *w*. Any possible confusion a beginner might have in distinguishing the *wh* from the separate consonants *w* and *h* may be avoided by teaching the words involved (*which, where, when,* and so forth) as sight words before either letter is used separately.

Initial	*Medial*	*Silent*	*Blends*
whatever	somewhat	who	bobwhite
why	meanwhile	whose	meanwhile
wherever	elsewhere	whole	overwhelm
wheat	pinwheel	whom	towhead
which	overwhelm	whoop	
whenever	bobwhite	whore	

The *th* sounds: For the beginning reader, the *th* combination approaches perfect coding. When the eyes focus on *th*, the teeth open slightly to permit the tip of the tongue to pass between, resulting in the production of one or the other of the two sounds. Which of the two sounds (*this* or *thin*) is produced will depend upon the other sounds involved. The sound to be spoken will be the one that is most easily articulated.

The *th* is silent in a few words (*isthmus*). When silent, inner speech ignores the silent letter, as all silent letters are ignored.

In compound words where *t* and *h* are together (*boathouse, masthead*), inner speech—the combined eye-mind-speech response—can furnish the reader with a word which fits the meaning of the sentence. If the word which is heard in the inner response is not in the vocabulary of the reader, help may be required to arrive at a satisfactory interpretation of the total meaning.

Initial	Medial	Final	Blends
the	weather	breathe	
that	either	with	
their	other	seethe	
these	bother	smooth	
thin	worthwhile	both	three
thing	mouthful	breath	throb
three	breathless	seventh	thrift
through	faithless	worth	thrill

The *sh* sound: This combination of two letters approaches perfect coding because the beginning reader can use the *sh* sound in recognition of the word both at its beginning and at its end. In the medial position there may be a prefix ending with *s* next to a word beginning with *h* (*dishonor, mishap*), resulting in loss of the *sh* sound. Inner speech will deal with such words as it does with compound words. The reader may need help in recognition of the word.

Initial	Medial	Final	Not the sh sound
she	sunshine	wish	dishonor
shrink	radishes	crush	
shall	finishing	finish	
shift	misshapen	fresh	mishap

The *zh* sound: The sound of *zh* (*Asia, occasion, azure*) not only has no letter in the alphabet but also has no two-letter combination to which it is assigned. It travels on letters which have plenty of sounds to represent without adding *zh* to their load. Its sound in some words easily becomes a *g* or a *j* (*garage, bon jour*).

The *ch* sound: The two-letter combination *ch* carries three possible pronunciations, as in *chin, chagrin,* and *chorus.* Of words like *chorus* some writers prefer to say that the *c* has the sound of *k* and the *h* is silent.

The *ch* may be located in any part of the word (*church, rancher, chagrin, machine, ache, choral, school*). A mature reader consults an authority when the correct pronunciation is needed, but beginners are dependent on a teacher. Such words, when they are met in the reading text, should be taught as sight words.

Sight words, when seen frequently enough while they are being pronounced, become tools of inner speech. The automatic sound response to needed words which contain the *ch* should be developed early.

ch as ch	*ch as k*	*ch as sh*	*ch blends*	*Final*
check	chorus	machine	intrench	watch
children	school	Chicago	pitcher	pitch
cheer		charade	church	church
cheese		chivalry	filching	hatch

The *ng* sound: The *ng* sound (*sing, singing*) is carried chiefly by the combination *ng*. It is also carried by *n* in many words (*ink, finger*). At the end of words, the *ng* is always the *ng* sound, but within words the two letters (*n* and *g*) create problems. The *n* may spell the *ng* sound or it may stand for the *n* sound, leaving the *g* to carry the sounds of *g* (*finger, strangler, stranger, unguarded, ingrowing*, and so forth).

The beginning reader has to be told the words; the mature reader may seek help from a dictionary.

However, after the learner has pronounced the words a few times with his eyes focused on them, his inner speech will produce the word for which the meaning calls.

ng as ng	*n as ng*	*n as ng, with g as g*	*No ng sound*
singing	ink (ingk)	finger (fing-ger)	ongoing
rang	thank	hunger (hung-ger)	ungraded
clanging	honk	angry (ang-gry)	engulf
clung	sunk	linger (ling-ger)	angel
hung	brink	bungler (bung-gler)	change
song	sink	strangler (strang-gler)	stranger
strength	drink	wrangler (wrang-gler)	plunge
wringer	wink	longer (long-ger)	twinge

The consonant blends

A consonant blend is two or more consonant letters with no vowel sound between them. The consonant blends so nearly approach perfect coding that only one initial combination (*sc*) is unreliable in the sense that when the eyes focus on the letters, the reader cannot be sure about the sounds involved. In *scald* and *scene* the *s* and the *c* are two consonants with no vowel in between, but when the *c* is silent there is no consonant with which to blend.

Blends with a final *s* at the end of words may use the sound of *z* instead of *s*; however, the reason for the *z* sound is the tendency in pronunciation of English words to take the easiest path. For example, *boyz* is much more easily articulated than *boyss*.

The letter *c* uses the *k* sound when blended with *l* or *r* (*class, crow*).

The *g* uses its *go* sound in all blends with *l* or *r* (*glass, grow*).

The blends of single letters with the two-letter sounds approach perfect coding (*match, phrase, shrill, earth, faithful, three, withstand, worthwhile,* and so forth).

With the five troublesome consonants (*c, g, h, s,* and *t*) thus approaching reliable coding in consonant blends, only the *x* and *y* and the two-letter sound *ng* (*sing, strange, strangle, think, thing*) remain serious threats to sounding by consonants as a dependable tool for word recognition.

CHAPTER II

INNER SPEECH

What should be printed in the blank spaces below?

Oh, say, can you _____
By the dawn's early _____
What so proudly _____ _____
At the twilight's last _____?
Jack and Jill went up the _____
To _____ _____ _____ _____ _____.
Jack fell _____
And broke _____ _____,
And Jill came _____ _____.

You undoubtedly recognized the opening lines of "The Star-Spangled Banner" and the nursery rhyme, and thereby found it easy to supply the missing words. The interesting fact about the performance, however, is that the missing words were not supplied by the eyes but by silent speech. In the first line, for example, it is improbable that you visualized the word *see* as it would appear in print had it been present. More than likely you supplied the word by an inner or silent pronunciation of the word without visualizing the printed word *see* at all.

This silent speech or inward pronunciation is inner speech.

Inner speech is the silent pronunciation of words that are already on file in the brain. For example, at the instant your eyes focused on the blank space at the end of the first line of "The Star-Spangled Banner," the word *see* came into your mind. The line "Oh, say, can you see" has been filed in your brain ever since you learned to sing the song; so that now when your eyes focused on the first part of the line, your inner speech produced the concluding word. If you had been listening to what was happening in your mind, you could have heard yourself say the entire line.

You can repeat the experience with the remainder of the lines of both the song and the nursery rhyme; and if you care to listen to what is happening in your mind, you can hear yourself sing the song or repeat the rhyme as you have sung or have said the words in the past.

In the same manner that the sight of the familiar words called up other words that have been filed in your brain, the individual letters can call up individual words. Note how you recognize the following words by pronouncing the consonants EVEN IN THE ABSENCE OF VOWEL LETTERS, except the silent e at the end of the word.

	r—m—mb—r	r—v—r
	n—mb—r	sp—d—r
sk—l—t—n	t—l—ph—ne	—r—thm—t—c
w—sd—m	t—l—gr—m	th——ght

Words are more easily recognized when in a meaning context, particularly words which have the same skeleton appearance, as below:

Yesterday he r—n a race.
Today he will r—n again.

He will s—ng a song.
He s—ng that song yesterday.
The s—ng he s—ng has been s—ng before.

He is a str—ng man.
He tied the parcel with a str—ng str—ng.

The meaning of the skeleton words may be quite different.

He did not feel w—ll. He w—ll feel w—ll now.
The boys w—re red sweaters. They w—re in this room.
Did you fly —v—r the high bridge? Did you —v—r fly before?

Inner speech in talk

Inner speech is a result of mental association between the muscles which control hearing and those which control speech. It has been operating in every individual who can hear ever since he learned to talk. It is a response whereby the mind can produce words; and if the individual can name the things on which his eyes are focused, he can hear an inner pronunciation of the words. It is an automatic response, quite as automatic as walking.

At first this inner response may be difficult to recognize. However, anyone who listens may hear it. He can hear it during the pauses which occur between the phrases and the sentences he is speaking. Furthermore, he can hear the pronunciation of one word or idea while he is speaking the words of another idea. He can hear himself repeating one set of numbers while he is dialing on a telephone another set of numbers. He can hear himself thinking the general meaning of a long sentence he is about to speak and at the same time he can be making decisions about the specific words he is to use, so that he hears only a few of them.

The moment a person centers his attention on his inner speech, the amount of inner response is likely to be increased and the rate of his thinking is likely to be reduced to the rate of speaking. One realizes how comparatively slow the rate of speaking is when it is compared with the rapid rate at which thinking may be done. It is possible for people to think so rapidly that the speech muscles cannot make all of the movements which the spoken words require. Then there is no inner response.

The absence of inner speech is easily observed when one is looking at a large number of things and begins to name only one of them. During the short time required to observe inner speech in connection with one thing, not only the observer recognizes all the others on which the eyes focus, but he can hear no inner pronunciation of any word other than the name of the one object to which he is giving attention.

As people talk, they have no concern about either the absence or the presence of the inner response, nor about alphabet letters and their sounds. They just use whatever words they have acquired in their vocabularies.

People who talk have no need for knowing that each word and every syllable of words carries a vowel element, or that all words, with the exception of the personal pronoun *I* and the indefinite article *a*, have at least one consonant letter. People may speak fluently without realizing the complexity of the process: how the fifteen specific vowels, the four diphthongs, and the dozens of spellings of the vowel sounds all are produced from one clear stream of breath as it emerges from the throat after having passed over the vibrating vocal cords; how the vibrating stream of tonal breath is modified in the mouth cavity as a result of the same movements (adjustments) which occur while the consonant sounds are being produced; how the vowel sounds are what they are because of the changes in the shape of the mouth cavity while the jaws open and partially or completely close, as the lips stretch and relax or open or close, as the tongue tenses and relaxes and changes shape, and as the soft palate either fits itself against the nasal passage, preventing the breath from emerging through the nose, or relaxes to allow all of it to go through the nasal passage to produce the three resonance sounds, the *m*, the *n*, and the *ng*.

To prove to yourself that the vowel sounds result from changes in the shape of the mouth cavity, observe what occurs while you say the word *remember*.

The tip of your tongue rises toward the top of your mouth to begin making the initial *r* sound. At the same time your lips begin to close. Between the *r* and the *m*, the escaping vibrating breath emerges and, because the shape of the mouth cavity is right for the neutral sound that is in the *rem* of *remember*, you hear the first part of the word.

While your lips are opening to provide for the second *m* of the accented syllable *mem*, your tongue and jaws are helping to make the exact shape of the mouth cavity to result in the sound of *e* that is in the accented syllable, and you can hear *remem*.

Your lips, lightly pressed together for the second *m*, have to press more tightly together to produce the sound of *b*; but to complete the sound of *b* your lips have to spring apart to emit a puff of breath, and you can hear the *mb* blend and *rememb*.

At the instant your lips open to complete the sound of *b*, the tip of your tongue begins to rise for the final *r*. During the interval between the sound of the *b* and the sound of the *r*, the outflowing vocalized breath is slightly obstructed by the rising tongue. The rising tongue cuts off the free-flowing vocalized sound, with the result that you can hear the neutral sound of the unaccented syllable *ber*.

Your speech machine made the three consonants correctly; and the different values of the vowel letter *e* were made in between the sounds of the consonants, r—m—mb—r. You must agree that the vowel values seemed to be produced almost as if by accident.

If you do not pronounce the final *r* of words, your tongue did not begin to rise after your lips parted to complete the sound of *b* but remained relaxed at the bottom of your mouth, so that the word you heard was *remembah*, for your inner speech treated the silent *r* as it treats all silent letters (as in *live, light, walk, pneumonia,* and *know*). Furthermore, if you habit is to add an r to some words (*law—lawr, idea—idear, area—arear, America—Americar*), you can hear the added sound of *r*.

Inner speech in reading

The inner sound response that can produce in the mind what is heard and can reproduce what the mind has already thought is the power which makes it possible for readers to use the sounds of the alphabet letters in learning new words and remembering those which they may have forgotten. Whereas for speaking mental association is between hearing and speech, for reading the association is between sight and thought. The eyes focus on the symbols and the mind thinks. This is the sight-mind response. Once the sight-mind associations have been

established, they act automatically whenever the situation calls
for their use. When this occurs, the sight-speech-mind takes
over temporarily, but only temporarily.

One of the important qualities of the automatic sound response is the way the speech muscles do not have to completely
articulate the sounds of the word. They may begin to sound the
word, but as soon as the mind has grasped the meaning and the
eye focus has moved away from the letters, the automatic sound
response is discontinued and the eyes and the mind go on working at the habitual rate.

There may or may not be inner speech during reading.
Whether there is will depend upon the habits which have been
learned in connection with word recognition and other phases
of the reading process.

The efficient habit is to look at the unknown word *only long
enough to recognize it* and then look away while making the
repetitions which may be needed to insure learning it.

If this procedure is always followed, the learner will be
spared the terrific job of breaking away from poor habits, such
as reading slowly word by word when there are many pages to
be read.

Inner speech in word recognition

Amazingly, whenever the skillful reader encounters an
unknown word, the sight-mind team stops with as much finality
as that with which electricity snaps off at the turn of a switch.
Instantly one of two things happens: either the eye focus leaps
across the difficult word and the reader's need is for the moment
satisfied by the context, or the sight-speech team takes over with
the inner sounding of the consonant letters. The reader hears
a word he has used in talk or has heard others use. If the word
fits into the meaning of the sentence, the sight-mind team takes
over again. However, if the reader hears an unfamiliar word
and cannot deduce the meaning from the context, he seeks help
from a dictionary or some other source.

A minimum of time is required for the switch from the rapid silent reading rate to the slower inner pronunciation, then back again to the rapid rate.

To more completely realize how this inner sound response operates, observe what happens when you, who are a skillful and therefore a rapid silent reader, encounter the last word of the sentence: "Very few people have ever seen a schistocephalus."

Unless you have used *schistocephalus* in talk or have seen it in print and are familiar with its meaning, you stop reading and begin to sound the first letters. Because you have seen and heard *sch* as *sk* in *school,* your inner speech will sound *sk.* Because a number of technical words begin with *schis* and are pronounced *skiz,* you may hear either *skiz* or *skiss.* Your eye focus will pass rapidly along the word toward the right and you will hear your automatic sound response producing the consonant sounds to the end of the word.

You did not consciously concern yourself with the sounds of the five vowel letters in the word because they posed no problem. Nor did you concern yourself about the syllables. Nevertheless, you divided the word into syllables according to your experience with words. You heard yourself say something comparable to *skis-to-sef-a-lus,* the dictionary pronunciation. (A schistocephalus is a deformed animal.)

Your inner speech was working for you, and working just as it has been serving you ever since you made the transition from memorized "sight'" learning to independent word recognition.

Note how this magical automatic sound response, this inner speech, makes it possible for beginners to read without having to be told each new word. Suppose *black* is an unknown word which the learners have used in talk but have not encountered in the reading text. Suppose also that the learners have had experience with the alphabet letters so that the sound response has been developed to *b, l,* and *k.* The instant the learners' eyes focus on the word, the speech muscles begin to articulate the sound of *b.* No pause will occur after the *b* sound because the eye habit is to move forward. Thus the speech muscles immediately become engaged in articulating the sound of the *l*, blending the two together in the way the consonants blend together in English words whenever there is no vowel sound between them. The eye focus passes over the vowel letter and the silent *c* and articulates the *k* sound. In inner speech, the readers hear *black*, and they use its meaning in the sentence.

Consonant framework of words

The following sentences showing words formed of consonant skeletons with dashes instead of vowel letters are readable. They illustrate how inner speech seems to deal with the consonant letters and does not concern itself with the vowels. The dash (—) in the consonant-skeleton words is a signal for the voweled breath to emerge between the consonants. Of course, since you are reading, you are seeking the meaning.

Th—y w—ll r—m—mb—r t— s—nd f—r th— b——k.
D—d sh— r—m—mb—r t— br—ng th— t—ck—ts?
Sh— d—d n—t th—nk —b— —t br—ng—ng th—m.
Th—t ch—ld w—s —n th—t c—ld r——m.
D—d y——r f—th—r g—t t— t—wn?
N—, b—t my m—th—r w—nt.
My m—th—r g—es t— t—wn t— sh—p.
My f—th—r g—es t— ch—rch t— l—st—n.
D—d y——r f—th—r f—nd h—s w—tch?
N—, h— d—dn't f—nd —t.
W— m—st b— v—ry qu——t —n th— h—sp—t—l.
Th— m—nk—ys j—mped fr—m tr—— t— tr——.
M—y w— h—ve th— pl——s—re —f y——r c—mp—ny?
W—ll th— m—n b— w—ll—ng t— s—— m—?
—s th—s th— n—nth —f N—v—mb—r?
N—, th—s —s n—t th— n—nth —f N—v—mb—r.
Th—s —s th— t—nth —f D—c—mb—r.

The words in the following sentences use no consonant letters except the nine (*b, k, l, m, q, r, v, w,* and *z*) which are

reliable in the sense that when the reader's eyes focus on them,
inner speech will produce their sounds. The only vowel letter
is the word *a*, pronounced as the first letter in *alone*, not as the
first letter of the alphabet.

B—ll w—ll k—ll a l—mb.
W—ll a z—br— b— w—rm?
M—mm— w—ll br——l l—v—r.
A w—rr——r w—ll w—lk —v—r a w—ll.

In the sentences which follow, no consonants other than the
nine reliables are used. The only vowel letters are the silent
e at the end of words and the first alphabet letter as it spells the
indefinite article, *a*.

K—rr—ll w—ll m—ke m—mm— a w—rm m——l.
A br——ze w—ll bl—w —v—r a w—ll.
M—ll—e w—ll br——l l—v—r —v—r a bl—ze.
W— l—ke a w—rm r——m.
L—ll——n w—ll l—ke a w—rkb——k.
W— b—l——ve B—ll—e w—ll l—ke a bl—e m—rble.
A br—ve w—rr——r w—ll —rr—ve.
M—z—e w—ll b——l m—re m—lk.
A r——m—r w—ll l—ke a w—rm r——m.
M—ke w—ll l—ke a br—wn br——m.

The two sounds of *th* (*this, thin*) are added to the nine
reliable consonants, the final silent *e*, and the indefinite article
in the following sentences.

Th— z—br— w—ll b— w—th th— l——n —r th— b——r.
Th— br——ze w—ll bl—w —v—r th— r—v—r.
M—th—r w—ll w—lk w—th th— —th—r br—th—r.
Ev—n th— w——l w—ll b— w—rm.
Th— br—th—r w—ll th—n b— w—rm.

The following sentences add the five letters (*d, f, j, n*, and
p) which are used for only two sounds each. Both of the sounds
are used in the same sentence. The second use of *j* is in foreign
words and they are capitalized.

d—t   D—v—d l——ked —n th— r——m —nd l—cked th—
          d——r.
f—v   F——r —f th— f—ve m—n —f B—st—n —re —ll.
j—   J—m J—nes j——ned J—s— F—rr—r n——r S—n J——n.
n—ng   N—n s—ng th— n—w s—ng f—r Fr—nk —nd F—rn.
p—ph   Ph—l—p ph—ned f—r th— p——n— pl—y—r.

The following sentences use the remaining seven letters
(*c, g, h, s, t, x,* and *y*), and the combinations in which the first
five (*c, g, h, s,* and *t*) help to spell the sounds *ch, sh, th, th, wh,*
and *ng.*

ng	W— c—n th—nk —b——t th— h—ng—ng g—rd—n.
wh(hw)	Wh—re —s th— wh—te wh—stle w— b——ght?
th	Thr—— th—rsty br—th—rs thr—w th— p—rty.
th	Th—s —s th— l—st tr—p w—th th—t br—th—r.
sh	Sh— s—rely l—kes s—g—r, —nd k——ps s—me —n h—r sh—p.
ch	H— g—es t— ch—rch —n Ch—c—g— —t Chr—stm—s t—me.
c	H— c—n —cc—pt th— p—ct—re —f th— pr—s—n c—ll.
g	Sh— c—n g—t th— g—m f—r th— g—ld r—ng.
h	H— h—s t— h—ve a h—t —n h—s h——d.
s	B—ys —nd g—rls s—— —s —se cr—y—ns.
t	Th—t tr—— w—ll —ttr—ct y——r —tt—nt——n.
x	Th— X-r—y m—ch—ne —s —t th— —x—t by th— xyl—ph—ne.
y	Y—s, th—y —re try—ng t— b—y l—vely y—ll—w m—ms.

Inner speech and silent letters

Silent letters are automatically ignored by the inner sound
response. This may be due to the fact that silent letters are
ignored in the spoken word, for it is unlikely that the inner
response will develop to letters which are not pronounced.

No rule accounts for the silent vowels with consistency.
Many words have two vowel letters with one of them silent
(*read, receive, oak, young, youth*). Hundreds of words have a

silent *e* at the end, but the *e* at the end of the definite article is
seen by the reader enough times to nullify any rule. (Four times
in the present sentence!)

Consonants seem to be silent because they are difficult to
pronounce (*know, write, gnaw, answer, through, enough, pneumonia, psychology, thumb, walk, listen, often*). Such letter combinations may at one time have been spoken.

In thousands of unaccented syllables the neutral vowel is
almost silent. Speakers use these unaccented syllables in speech
without concern as to their spelling. It is the writers who have
to know which of the vowel letters is needed, for the vowel may
be any one of the five (*forward, taken, pencil, lemon, circus*).

Note how readable the sentences are with silent letters pre-
dominating in the words.

L–st n–ght th– m–n th––ght th–y w–––ld g– thr–––gh
w–th th– –r–g–n–l pl–n. Th–y s–––d, th–––gh, th–t th–y
sh–––ld h–ve –n–––gh c–m–nt –n h–nd t– c–mpl–tely
c–v–r th– sh–––ld–rs –f th– h–ghw–y.

Inner speech that is harmful

The power of the muscles to produce the words during
reading is fine for word recognition. It is due to this power that
we can recognize words through the process of sounding. However, there is danger lest the automatic sound response become
overdeveloped to the extent that the beginner may become the
victim of exaggerated inner speech and will pronounce the
words he is reading.

Exaggerated inner speech results from keeping the eyes
focused on the words while pronouncing them. When the eye
focus remains on the word, the associations between the sight
and the sound (the sight-speech associations) become stronger
than is needed for sufficient automatic sound response. Efficient
reading requires the sight-mind associations to be stronger than
the sight-speech associations. Owing to the fact that associations
between the spoken word and its meaning have existed since

early childhood, there is a strong affinity between the sight of the new word and its familiar sound. In consequence, with a minimum of opportunity the inner speech (sight-sound) associations will become stronger than the sight-mind associations.

For this reason, unless preventive measures are strictly adhered to, the well-developed sight-sound response which produces the spoken word when the eyes focus on it is likely to take precedence over the newly developing sight-mind response which produces the meaning at the instant the eyes focus on the words, as it has to occur in efficient reading. When the sight-speech response takes precedence over the sight-mind response, the reader pronounces the words before he secures their meaning.

Why inner speech is effective

The miraculous way in which all learners could use—and all efficient readers do use—the sounds of the seemingly unphonetic letters of the alphabet is due largely to the following factors:

1. Inner speech is a part of the mental-physical equipment of every individual who sees and hears and thinks and in consequence speaks. It first enables him to speak his thoughts; then, after he begins learning to read, it enables him to achieve independent word recognition and to continue toward efficient and effective reading.

2. The diverse spelling of the neutral vowel in the thousands of unaccented syllables of words (*alone, taken, pencil, lemon, circus*), with all of the vowel letters representing the same sound, contributes to belief in the futility of being concerned about the specific sounds which the vowel letters represent in words.

3. The English language intonation, with its characteristic stressing of one syllable in each thought-phrase, which results in partial neutralization of many full-value vowel letters, adds to the certainty that the specific sound of the vowel letters is not really important. (See *Reading Can Be Fun*, by Henderson.)

4. The way that inner pronunciation follows the pattern of

vocal speech by passing rapidly over unstressed words and syllables and totally ignoring silent letters is further evidence that the specific vowel sound is relatively unimportant.

5. Teachers can control the type and amount of automatic sound response. They can control both type and amount by seeing to it that the learners look at the printed word only long enough for the sight-meaning associations to be made, and that they then look away from the text while additional repetitions are being made. When this is done, a sufficient amount of sight-sound association will be made. Later, when the reader's eyes focus on the text, the meaning will come first; the sound will come as an additional response and will be present only when it is needed for a definite purpose, either to aid in word recognition or for one of the types of oral reading.

6. Reliability and stability of the consonant letters and combinations of consonant letters, coupled with the lack of reliability and lack of stability characteristic of the vowels, account for the usefulness of inner-speech phonics.

7. Yet another factor is important: the tendency of English-speaking people to accept the easiest possible pronunciations, with the result that many of the vowel sounds seem to be produced almost accidentally in between the mouth and tongue adjustments that are needed in producing the consonant sounds.

Inner speech in advertising

Modern advertising is utilizing the automatic sound response. It is demonstrating the power of inner speech. Not all of us realize our indebtedness to Benjamin Franklin, who went out into the storm with his kite and his key. Certainly he did not foresee that his experiment would grow into a stupendous advertising medium.

In the beginning, advertisers utilized only the spoken word, but now they not only have it said, they have it sung. Moreover, it is being said and sung over and over again and again, sometimes so off-key that we shudder at the unpleasantness. We have been—and are being—bombarded with tunes and slogans until a theme tune or key word or slogan sets up such a chain reaction that our inner speech immediately produces the name of the product and the company, and we find ourselves singing the commercials, and, of course, we buy the products.

Inner speech, which is meant to be in evidence only when there is some use for it, is now an inner command to buy the only—and always new or improved or safe—this or that. Big-name entertainers advise us, confident that we will surely take what they (and a high percentage of the doctors!) take or pre-scribe in order to be fit or "safe" for the next day's work or play.

Advantages to be had from inner speech

People who are interested in awakening the interest of educators in the value of inner speech might with profit induce some big-name entertainer to sing about the advantages we al-ready enjoy because of this inner response.

An entertainer might be willing to remind us that his own inner speech is to a large extent responsible for additions to his vocabulary because he uses the new words in imaginary talks with his friends. He could tell how he memorizes quickly be-cause he knows how to make repetitions in his inner speech, how he can try out different interpretations and then decide which will be the most effective.

He could affirm that his appreciation and pleasure in poetry and rhythmic prose are due to his inner speech.

The entertainer might even be willing to sing about how he worked himself out of reading "improvement'" classes and thereafter steadily advanced to success. Furthermore, he might be anxious to tell how this way of sounding words had enabled his young son to avoid having to be demoted to a remedial class to learn what he might have learned during his first year at school.

CHAPTER III

PHONICS

The use that is made of the alphabet letters and their sounds is called "phonics." If people are reading—or if they are teaching others to read—they are making use of the sounds of the letters in the words. All readers who have become able to recognize words without having to be told them are using phonics. If no teacher has taught it to them, they have worked out a system for themselves. Such is—and has always been—the situation no matter what method seems to have been followed while people have been learning to read.

Historians have described three rather distinct "methods" whereby people have been taught to read: the alphabet, sight learning, and phonics.

With the alphabet method, the learners were taught their "letters" before they were expected to begin reading. Their attention was focused on the letters of each new word. Because they could name the letters, they were also learning to spell the words. To be able to spell was of value and posed no difficulty, for no beginning words had more than three or four letters. Another advantage of the alphabet method was that the learners were developing the inner sound response to the letters, so that when their eye focus passed along the word from letter to letter in the left-to-right direction, the speech muscles would produce the word and the learners would pronounce it either aloud or in inner speech. Furthermore, some of the new words were first seen on a page with a picture of the thing that was being named. When the learners saw the word and the picture at the same instant, associations were being made between the muscles which control sight and meaning. Thus they were learning by the sight-to-meaning route. Then, while they were making the repetitions of the word and at the same time were looking at it, associations were being made between the three sets of muscles—sight, meaning, speech—and the inner sound response was developing into inner speech.

The weakness of the alphabet method was that too much automatic sound response was developed to the vowel letters, which are used in more than a hundred different spellings, and to the seven consonants (*c, g, h, s, t, x,* and *y*), which are used in at least forty different ways. Moreover, too much attention to the letters while the eyes remained on the words resulted in word-by-word silent reading. In consequence, the reading rate was limited to the rate of pronunciation.

The best thing about the sight method was the way learners were taught to see the words as wholes. At the same time, the meaning was closely tied to the word by the direct route for efficient reading, in which the reader thinks the meaning at the instant his eyes focus on the symbols. With this method, the learners looked at the words, used them over and over again, and remembered them. The readers could gain a sight vocabulary without delay and thereby begin at once to realize the advantages and pleasure which result from being able to read. Moreover, even though they may not have been conscious of it, the automatic sound response to many whole words was developing. This was particularly advantageous with unphonetic words which are not easily learned through sounding (*know, right, enough, thought, could, shoulder, though, through,* and so forth).

The weakness of the sight method was its failure to use the sounds of the phonetically reliable letters in word recognition, with the result that when the sight load became over-heavy, the learners were unable to cope with it and became potential dropouts or members of remedial reading classes.

The best thing about the phonics method was its use of the sounds of the consonant letters as aids in independent word recognition. Its weakness was its attention to rules which were rendered useless by exceptions. Young children who could not understand abstract terms were taught to recite rules and were more puzzled than helped by the exceptions. A child who was taught the "family" at the end of *cat* and *pat* and *rat* and *sat* wanted also to sound the family in *what*. A child who recited, "When two vowels come together, the first does the talking and the other goes a-walking," had questions instead of help when he encountered words like *eight* and *oasis* and *read* in the past tense. To know the rule about *save* and *five* was less than helpful to a child who was already seeing *have* and *live*. A list ending *ow* (*cow, now, how*) was disturbing to a thinking child when he saw words with the same ending (*snow, grow, row*) pronounced differently.

Phonics is presented here as a system rather than as a method. It is assumed that phonics experiences for all beginners are essentially the same regardless of their age. The difference lies mainly in their level of maturity. It is largely a matter of making sure that all members of the learning group know all of the alphabet letters and are making all of the consonant sounds correctly.

If all members of the group are making the consonant sounds correctly, they can eventually learn to make the vowel sounds. The vowel sounds are what they are because of changes which are made in the shape of the mouth cavity. During the instant that any vowel sound is being spoken, all of the breath stream is flowing unobstructed past the vibrating vocal cords and through the mouth cavity. In the mouth it is manufactured into vowel sounds. The specific sound it is to be, is determined by the size and shape of the oral cavity. The changes in size and shape are brought about by adjustments which occur in the four parts of the speech machinery, the jaws, the lips, the tongue, and the velum.*

The adjustments which occur while the vowels are being

---

* For more detail, see Ellen C. Henderson, *Reading Can Be Fun* (New York: Exposition Press, 1956), p. 116.

produced obstruct the breath, with the result that the consonants are what they are.

The English language has only twenty-five consonants, each
of which is made by its own definite adjustments. This is not
true of the vowels. The fifteen cardinal vowels are not always
spoken as definite sounds. Many of them have a diphthongal
quality comparable to what occurs in the four diphthongs (*oi-
oy, ou-ow, i, u*), so that we can hear a double sound making the
a in *ate* into what may be spelled by adding a second letter
(*a-e*). While the vowels are being produced, the tongue may
not hold its position firmly to the end of the sound but may
shift its pressure, rising slightly or relaxing or falling to a neutral
position.

These various movements occur while words are being pronounced. Notice what happens while you pronounce *skeleton*.
The initial consonants blend. The tongue relaxes from its *k*-
position to let its tip go to the *l*-position. The tongue has to relax
before it can increase the pressure behind the teeth to make the
needed sound of *t*. It has to move back from the *t*-position before it can assume the *n*-position. The vowel sounds seem to
make themselves while the tongue is doing its work. The first *e*
receives its cardinal value. The second *e* and the *o* receive a
mere touch of sound—the same vowel value in both.

The same thing that happens while the word is being pronounced occurs while the eyes focus on the letters. In oral pronunciation the stimulus is the intention of the speaker. In
reading, the stimulus is sight. For the sightless the stimulus is
touch. Reading power results from associations between the
mind and sight—or touch—and speech. It may be that the importance of speech in the reading process is due to the fact that
most people are speaking before they begin to learn to read.
Regardless of the reason, the eyes focus on the letters, and the
speech muscles can produce the sounds. However, the speech
machinery seems to be tied more closely to the constant consonants than to the variable vowels. This is not surprising, for there
is a wide difference between twenty-one symbols representing
twenty-five consonant sounds and five letters representing a

hundred sounds. Anyway, the consonants seem—like skeletons—to sustain the vowels.

While becoming able to read efficiently, people develop through five stages of phonics training:

1. Readiness—knowing the alphabet and making the sounds correctly.
2. The memorization period of sight learning.
3. Transition from sight learning to independent word recognition.
4. Independent word recognition and wide reading.
5. Preparation for dictionary pronunciation.

STAGE ONE
The Alphabet

Because phonics is the use of the sounds of the letters in learning to read, the logical place to start is with the alphabet. The training has already begun when the learner first focuses his eyes on a known symbol while he is speaking its name. The three-way associations that begin to be made develop to become the automatic sound response. Individuals who know the alphabet have already developed the inner speech response to the twenty-three letters which carry the sound in the name of the letter. The three letters which do not carry their sounds in their names are the *w*, the *h*, and the *y*. Six of the consonant sounds are missing. Four of the missing sounds are the *go* sound of *g*, the *ng* (*sing, think*), the *sh* (*she, sure*), and the *zh* (*measure, azure*). However, the four are produced by the same adjustments which occur when other sounds are produced; for the *g* and *ng* adjustment is the same as that for the *k*, and the *sh* and *zh* adjustment is the same as that for the *j* and *h*. The one adjustment that is missing from the names of the letters is the thrust of the tip of the tongue for the two *th* sounds (*this, three*).

These six sounds should be used in talk so that every member of the learning group will be hearing them. In the second stage, they will be used in sentences. Simple sentences for talk are:

She will go with us.
The sky is azure blue.
This is a pleasure trip.
The three girls are singing.

More than half of the vowel sounds occur in the names of the letters. The names of five (*a, e, i, o, u,*) carry three of the cardinal vowels (*a, e,* and *o*) and two of the diphthongs (*i* and *u*). A second sound of the letter *e* is used in the names of several letters (*f, l, m, n, s, x*). Another sound of *i* is in the name of *k* (*kai*). The sound of *oo* in *room* is in the name of three letters (*q, u,* and *w*). Another sound of the letter *a* is in the name of the letter *r* (*ahr*). One of the sounds of the diphthong *i* is the *a* in *ask*. A second sound of the letter *u* (*up*) is in the first syllable of the *w*. The neutral vowel is in the second syllable of *w*. The vowel sounds which do not occur in the names of the letters are in the words *cat, air, arm, water, corn, word,* and *book.* Of the missing vowels, the sound in *at* may need much practice. Many speakers fail to open the jaws wide enough. People who make the *i* in *it* sound instead of the *e* in *end* in common words (*pen, pencil, tend, attend*) should practice opening the jaws wider.

The next stage in the learning-to-read process should not be attempted until *every member of the learning group* is able to point to and name all of the alphabet letters. The time spent in waiting for individuals to catch up is not wasted. Those who seem to know the most may be taught how to help others. In any event, no one should be permitted to fail. At this stage of learning, every person who can see and hear can learn.

STAGE TWO
Phonics in Memorization
(Sight Learning)

Phonics training in the sight learning period is a continuation of development of the automatic sound response to the letters and combinations of letters that occur in the vocabulary of the sentences and other texts that are used while beginners are learning to read.

The three letters (*h, w,* and *y*) which do not carry their name sound in the alphabet should receive immediate attention. The automatic sound response to the three may be begun with the sentence "*What is your name?*" The two letters *wh* should be named together, not *w* and *h* separately. The eyes focus on the *wh* but inner speech produces *hw,* the sound sequence that is used in all words in which *wh* occurs. Inner speech follows the pattern of the speaker. In the sentence the *y* is used in its initial position, where the *y* is always the sound of *y*.

The one adjustment which is missing from the names of the alphabet should receive immediate attention. Because the two letters (*t* and *h*) spell a consonant sound, they should be spoken of as the *th* letters. Such sentences as "*This is your name. This is my name. There are three books,*" afford the repetitions that are needed.

To avoid confusion, the learners should develop the automatic sound response to two more combinations which spell consonant sounds (the *ph* and the *sh*) before they see the *p* and the *s* in words.

Talk about the letters is important. For one thing, during talk about the letters the inner sound response continues on its way toward becoming automatic. For this reason, the two letters of each of the two-letter sounds (*ch, sh, th, th, wh, ng*) should be kept a unit. For example, saying "The *wh* at the beginning of that word" keeps the two letters a unit. Letters that should be used before others are the consonant combinations which spell the sounds at the beginning of *what, this, three, she,* and *phrase.* Words using these two-letter sounds should be taught before the learners are taught words containing the individual letters (*w, h, t, s, p*).

This is important, for unless sufficient automatic response to the two-letter sounds has been developed, beginners may try to use the single letters instead of the two-letter sounds. This might easily occur because in early experience with the alphabet letters the inner sound response to *p, s,* and *t* is developed.

The experience sentences should use words with letters which are phonetic in that they represent only their own sound. These are *b, k, l, m, q, r, v, w,* and *z* (except in a very few words) and the two-letter sounds *wh, ph,* and the two *th* sounds. A few others always represent their alphabet sounds in specific word positions. These at the beginning of words are *d, f, h, n, y,* and *z* and at the end of words *n, p,* and *sh.* The letter *s* is needed in early sentences, both as the sound of *z* (*is*) and as its alphabet sound (*this*). Beginners will have no trouble remembering the two words (*this, is*) if they develop the inner sound response to them in the sentence "*This is my name.*" The *n* may be used (*name*) before the *ng* because at the beginning and at the end of words, the *n* is always its name-sound (*no, in, none*), and the *n* of the *ng* is always within the word.

All vowel letters may be used. In sight words—and before there is talk about sounds—the vowels are a part of the word and the words should be seen as wholes. If someone asks about the sound of a vowel, the answer should be, "That letter has one of the sounds of . . ." and the letter named.

While the beginners are talking about the letters in words and before they begin to talk about sounds, some of the sight words used should begin with the following letters:

1. The *c,* using the sound of *k.* The alphabet name-sound of *c* (*s*) is used in only a few of the early words whereas the sound of *k* is used in many.
2. The *g,* using the sound in *go.* The new automatic sound response to the *g* should be developed before the *j* sound

is even stronger than it has already become while the beginner has been looking at *g* and making the *j* sound.

3. The *k* with its silent use (*know, knew, knee*). Given a chance, the inner sound response to such words as these will develop as they are pronounced in vocal speech, *n* with silent *k*.

4. The *x*, using two of its sounds: the *gz* (*exit*) and the *ks* (*six*).

5. The *j*, before the learner sees words such as *San Juan, José*.

6. The *y* at the beginning of words (*your*) and in its uses of the sounds of the vowel letter *i* (*my, try, trying, baby, lovely*).

Beginners should learn unphonetic words during the memorization stage (*enough, know, write, laugh, laughed, right, thought, through*).

Talk about the sounds in words may begin as soon as the learners show interest. Adults realize that the letters represent sounds, but children have to learn through experiences which have significance to them.

Teachers can awaken interest. Whatever the age of the learners, the teacher has to keep a record of attendance. A filing system affords talk about the sounds at the beginning of the pupils' names.

Use the letter *m* to begin talking about the sounds in words. In the first place, there will be a name which begins with *m*: if no member of the class has an *m* name, the teacher's *Miss* or *Mrs.* or *Mr.* will serve. In the second place, the *m* sound is made correctly much more easily than otherwise. The speakers can feel the vibration at the closed lips, and they can know that the lips remain closed until the sound is completed. Thus there will be no possibility of an added vowel sound.

An ideal sentence will repeat the sound. A good one for adults is: "*Mack's mother may be in the room.*" A good one for children is: "*My mamma may be in the room.*"

Any individual who talks about the language sounds should realize that although the sounds may be described and produced, no combinations of letters may be written to represent the actual sounds. For example, the sound of *b* occurs in *b*'s alphabet name; but the name of the letter uses a vowel sound, and the name of the letter with an *e* sound added becomes *be* or *bee* or *Bea*. Again, when anyone says "the *a* sound," a listener may wonder which of the nine sounds of *a* is meant.

Although some of the sounds are easily produced in isolation, others are very difficult to make without adding a vowel sound (*buh, guh, uhl, er, wuh,* and so forth).

The safe way to speak of sounds is to say "the sound of *b*" or even "the *b* sound" if no attempt is made to make the sound.

Reference to a vowel sound should not be made in terms of "short" or "long." The two words describe only two of the numerous sounds of each vowel letter. It is better to say, "the sound of *a* that is in *that*," or "the sound of *a* that is in *what*." "Short" should be applied to both; but dictionaries mark them differently. The sound of *o* in *rode* is no "longer" than the vowel in *room*.

Words lists should be kept and made available to members of the class at all times. With such lists the students can make comparisons between the new words and those which are already listed.

The lists may be of words which are alike in some way, with the same initial consonant letters or the same consonant blends or perhaps the same consonant letters but with different vowel letters.

No attempt should be made to list words by "families" only. Adults might be able to cope with the exceptions but a child may be merely puzzled or discouraged. A child who was compiling words ending with the "*at*" family wanted to know how to pronounce *hat* with a *w* in front of it (*what*).

After each discussion of a sound in a word, the members of the class should offer other words containing the sound. From the words contributed, the teacher should select those that had been—or would be—in the reading vocabulary, and should print them in columns either on a bulletin blackboard or on strips of oaktag so that other words may be added. The words should be

printed with the vowel letters that use the same vowel sound—
and the letter *y* where it uses one of the sounds of the letter *i*—
underneath the letter of the matching sound even though the
letters which represent the vowels are not the same.

Such lists as these eliminate vowel duplication and ambigu-
ity without making a point of inconsistencies or overlapping. At
the same time they focus the attention on the vowel sounds with,
however, the additional value of their being produced between
the consonants in the same way that they are used by inner
speech.

Eventually the lists look much like the table shown on the
facing page.

The lists make no provision for some of the commonly used
sounds. However, in the beginning no attempt should be made
to plan space for each of the fifteen vowels, the four diphthongs,
and the neutral vowel. At first there would be only a few vowel
sounds. The columns might be shortened by the removal of well-
known words and space made available by the removal of columns no longer needed. No beginner need be bothered by such
details as that the letter *a* has nine sounds (*at, ate, air, ask,
father, war, daughter, earn, alone*) or that the letter *o* has ten
sounds (*on, old, son, corn, room, look, word, lemon, out, oil*)
and is used in more than thirty different ways.*

---

* The uses of the letter *o* are *oasis, old, road, though, shoulder,
soldier, snow; on, gone, thought, solder; one, son, enough, does,
other; look, could; room, through, to, two, buoy; oil, boy, buoyant;
out, how, drought; lemon; word, colonel; Ouija board.*

this	name	book	phone	room
is	eight	look	old	to
in	late	looked	cold	zoo
did	face	took	fold	school
thing	wait	could	shoulder	ruler
think	Grace	sugar	grow	her
six	Amos	sure	snow	word
live	Ada			were
going		up	go	church
trying	five	does	going	first
bring	alive	under	over	
	my	come	eat	on
out	try	one	feet	gone
brown	trying		see	thought
how	I	boy	me	father
now	ice	toy	we	always
sound	light	Roy	three	
	write		be	
	bright			

STAGE THREE

Transition From Sight Learning to
Independent Word Recognition

In the third stage of phonics training, the learners begin to "sound" the words. Adults reach this stage rather early in their learning-to-read experiences; young children require time enough for many repetitions to be made. Adults can take short cuts and quickly accomplish what they have to do in order to learn; young children have to follow the guidance of teachers, step by step.

Two procedures must be followed by both adults and children. Learners must let the eye focus pass rapidly from left to right along the word while their speech mechanism is producing the sounds. And they must be concerned primarily with the meaning of the sentence of which the unknown word is a part. In other words, the eyes and the mind must work together.

Adults may need to learn new habits to replace word-by-word silent reading in which they keep the eyes focused on the words and pronounce each one. Children can learn the rapid left-to-right eye-mind habit at the beginning.

Adults can understand the mechanics of the inner pronunciation. They can realize that the vowel letters represent many different sounds. They can observe what is occuring inside their mouths when the vowel sounds are being produced. They can believe that the vowel letters within the words are signals for the jaws or lips to separate to make way for the breath needed for good vowel production and for the tongue to do its important work.

Children do not need to know the reasons. What they have to do is follow the lead of their teachers. They have only to see the words and know what the words are telling them.

The teachers need to be sure that the inner sound response to the letters which are always the same sound in all word positions—*b, l, m, q, r, v, z, wh, th, th*—has been developed. After the *wh* has been used, the *w* becomes one of the reliables because, although *w* is silent in some words (*answer, know, saw*), it is never used to represent any other sound. The *k* also is reliable in the sense that it is never used to represent any sound other than the *k*. Moreover, the *f* would be one of the reliables if the little word *of* were spelled as it sounds, *ov*.

Add *d, f, h,* and *n* to the list of reliables at the beginning of words. Others which are always their own sound at the end of words total nineteen: *b, h, j, k, l, m, n, p, r, v, w, x, z, wh, th, th, sh, ph, ng.*

Beginners are in the transition stage when they discover that they can know the new word by sounding the consonants from left to right.

Adults make the discovery early in the sight-learning stage. Children need not be conscious of what is occurring, although some of them may become so.

Whenever help is needed, it should be offered. Unobtrusive help should be given in the same way regardless of the age of the group, except that more time will be needed for the young children than is needed for individuals who are older.

The teacher's preparation is largely a matter of selecting a word which is in the vocabulary of the learners. For example, if *ribbon* is a new word in a sentence which is being read, the teacher might say to the reader, "Instead of telling you what the word is, I'll help you sound through it the way I do when I come to a word I don't know. I'm not going to ask someone who knows the word to tell it. You watch what I'm going to do to show you how to help yourself learn a new word.

"I'll put three words you know on the chalkboard, with their letters spread apart.

r e d   b o o k   r u n

"You see my hand under the *r* of *red*. I'll make the sound of *r*, then I'll pass my hand quickly across the *e* and hold it under the *d*. Now I'll say the word while I'm moving my hand from the *r* to the *d*.

"I'll say the word again. This time I'll hold my hand under the *r* long enough for you to see that the tip of my tongue is raised toward the top of my mouth. When I move my hand quickly across the *e*, you can see that my tongue will come down from the top of my mouth and then go back up to touch just behind my upper teeth. I'll say the word again in a sort of slow motion. I'll not be able to hold my tongue after I begin to sound the *r*, because the sound of *r* at the beginning of a word hasn't begun until the tongue starts to come downward. So, as soon as I feel my tongue come downward, I'll move my hand quickly across the *e* to the *d*. Now, let's all say *red* together while my hand moves underneath the letters.

"Now let's do the same with *book*. My hand will move across both of the *o*'s because they spell one sound in this word.

"Let's do the same with *run*.

"I'll print these three words again and erase the vowel letters, but put a dash instead of the vowel letters. Then we'll sound through the three words.

r—d

b——k

r—n

"I'll print the word some of you hadn't recognized when I stopped you. Please don't even whisper the word if you recognize it while I'm printing it.

ribbon

"Now I'll print it underneath with dashes instead of vowel letters.

"When you see any of these vowel letters in a word, you need to be sure you are letting your tongue do what it has to do to make the consonant sounds.

"Now I'll print the word. You see two *b*'s in the middle; but you won't use both of them. There is no vowel letter between them to use up the puff of breath with which a sound of *b* has to finish. So the first *b* is silent.

"Let's all of us sound through the word while my hand moves along the letters.

"You hear yourself say *ribbon*. Now read the sentence silently, then we'll all read aloud."

This is the process. It works in ninety-eight per cent of the words in our language.

The teacher pronounces unphonetic words or says, "The vowel letter in this word has the sound you can hear in . . . Let's put that sound in."

The following information may enable teachers to give assistance to learners who do not make the language sounds correctly:

The fifteen distinct vowel sounds result from changes in the shape of the mouth cavity while the breath is coming from the lungs through the mouth, where the changes in shape are occurring owing to the obstructions which are set up by the various parts of the speech machine. The four diphthongs (*i, u, oi-oy, ou-ow*) are blendings of vowel sounds.

The twenty-five consonant sounds are given here alphabetically.

b: To make the sound of *b*, press the lips together lightly and listen for the tone which results from vibration of the vocal cords and the lips. Notice that there is a steady pressure. The pressure and the vibration do not complete the sound of *b* until the lips open for a puff of breath. There is no vowel sound unless the next letter carries a vowel sound. Notice what happens while you say *box* or *bug*. Then say *blue*. The puff of breath precedes the sound of *l* and blends with it.

ch: To make the *ch* sound (*church*), slightly round and protrude the lips, close the teeth, and press the tongue against them. The teeth spring slightly apart to let the breath explode.

d: The sound of *d* is made with the front of the tongue back of the upper front teeth while the jaws are open at least a fourth of an inch. Whether the jaws are open or closed, the tongue makes its characteristic movement.

f: The sound of *f* is made with the lower lip slightly under the upper teeth. Breath emerges between the edge of the teeth and the lower lip.

g: The sound of *g* is made with the back part of the tongue raised and pressed against the front part of the soft palate. This rising of the tongue is a sort of bunching backward. The nasal passage is blocked, thus forcing all of the breath to emerge through the mouth. The vocal cords are vibrating and the throat muscles exert pressure, the evidence of which is easily observed or even felt when the hand is placed against the throat.

h: The sound of *h* is just breath. It is always made in conjunction with the vowel sound that follows, as in *have,* or with the sound of *w,* as in *what* (*hwat*).

j: The sound of *j* is made like the sound of *ch,* with the lips slightly rounded and protruded. The teeth are together and the tongue is pressed against them. The teeth spring apart and the tongue is so unwilling to remove itself to let the vibrating breath emerge that we almost—but not quite—hear a sound of *d* in conjunction with the *j.*

k: The sound of *k* is made very much like the sound of *g* except that the vocal cords are not vibrating, so that only breath is expelled. Movement of the throat muscles is even more in evidence than for the *g* sound.

l: The sound of *l* is made by touching the front of the tongue lightly behind the upper front teeth while vibrating breath is emerging.

m: The sound of *m* is made with the lips pressed together lightly and vibrating slightly while the vocal cords are vibrating and all of the breath is emerging through the nasal passage. The *m* is one of the three sounds (*m, n,* and *ng*) which are responsible for resonance in the voice.

n: The sound of *n* is made with the tongue fitted tightly against the upper gum to prevent the vibrating breath from emerging through the mouth. When even a small amount of breath escapes over the side of the tongue, the voice takes on a semi-nasal quality which is referred to as the "nasal" voice. The *n* is one of the three sounds which are responsible for resonance in the voice.

ng: The *ng* sound is made with the back of the tongue raised toward the top of the mouth as for the sounds of *g* and *k*. However, the soft palate relaxes to insure free passage of the vocalized breath through the nose. If any of the breath escapes through the mouth, the voice takes on an unpleasant nasal quality. The *ng* is the third sound to add resonance to the voice. The three are easily practiced in *morning*.

p: While the sound of *p* is being produced, the lips are closed and pressed together, but they immediately open to emit a puff of breath. There is no voice. The sound which follows the sound of *p* may be either another consonant (*play*) or a vowel (*paper*) or the beginning of another word (*upstairs*).

r: The sound of *r* is made with the jaws open enough for the tip of the tongue to rise toward the top of the mouth. If the tongue does not rise, a listener hears either a substitution such as is made in infant speech (*wabbit, wubbuh, fathah, bwothah,* and so forth) or a dialect (*cah, fathah, brothah,* and so forth). After the tongue-tip has risen to make the *r* sound, it immediately drops back down as if to be ready for the sound which is to come next. Sometimes the next sound is another *r* (*hurry, carry, car runs,* and so forth).

s: The sound of *s* is made while the unvocalized breath, which is emerging through a groove in the center of the tongue, is obstructed by closed teeth. During the production of the *s* sound, the tongue is fitted tightly at the sides, preventing breath from escaping to result in a "lateral *s*," a serious speech "defect."

sh: The *sh* sound is made with the lips slightly rounded and protruded. The teeth are together and the tongue is relaxed from an *s* position. The breath, unvocalized, emerges in a steady stream.

t: The sound of *t* is made with separated teeth and the tongue pressed lightly but closely against the inside of the upper jaw. The unvocalized breath is momentarily held above the tongue. The tongue suddenly drops, and the breath escapes with a sharp explosive sound.

th: Both of the *th* sounds (*this, thin*) are made with the tip of the tongue between the teeth. For the voiced sound (*this*), the speaker can feel vibration of the tongue. For the other sound (*thin*), the breath seems to be forced from the front of the tongue.

v: The *v* sound is the twin of the sound of *f*. The lower lip is slightly under the upper teeth. The vocal cords are vibrating and the speaker can feel vibration of the lip against the teeth.

w: While the sound of *w* is being produced, the lips are closed but not pressed together. The vocal cords are vibrating and the speaker can feel vibration of the lips. When the lips do not meet (*saw, answer*), the vocal cord vibration is lacking and there is no *w* sound.

wh: The sound of *h* (just emerging breath) precedes the sound of *w*. As the jaws close after having been apart for emergence of the breathy *h*, the lips close. The speaker can hear the tonal vibration and feel the vibration of the lips.

y: The sound of *y* is made with separated teeth and the sides of the tongue pressed against the upper teeth. The middle of the tongue is raised to form an obstruction to the stream of vocalized breath that is passing over the arched tongue. The lips are stretched from side to side. The *y* sound is easily produced after the sound of *e* in *eat*.

z: The sound of *z* is made while the vocalized breath emerges over the tongue in a steady stream. The speaker can feel tongue vibration.

zh: The *zh* sound is the twin sound of the unvocalized *sh* sound. It is never spelled by *zh* but by *s* or *z* as in *occasion, decision, measure, pleasure, azure* and *seizure*.

STAGE FOUR

Independent Word Recognition

When the learners have become able to help themselves, they are well on their way toward independent word recognition. By this time, adults are also well on the way toward making use of the dictionary for both pronunciation of words and to understand the meaning.

Children will have had so much experience with filing that they can open their alphabet pages to a specific letter without having to rattle off the letters in sequence.

People of any age will have reached this stage through having learned to seek help when they meet a problem. Moreover, they will have had experiences which have resulted in the following:

1. Realization that letters are symbols of sound in words.
2. Knowledge of the alphabet to enable them to use the letters as clues for memorization.
3. Maintenance of the rapid left-to-right movement of the eye focus along the line of print.
4. Development of the automatic sound response to the reliable consonants.
5. Reliance on inner speech while sounding through an unknown word.
6. Substitution of other letters—and sounds—when the inner-speech word is not easily recognized.
7. Comparison of words or parts of words with other words or parts of words.
8. Skill—or judgment, perhaps—in trying out a second or third sound of a letter—or combination of letters—when the inner-speech word does not fit the meaning of the sentence.

Such trials concerning the nine (b, k, l, m, q, r, v, w, and z) which are used to represent any sound other than their own—excepting z in rare words—consist in testing for silent letters. This is not difficult because silent letters are ignored by inner speech just as they are ignored in oral speech.

Trials for the five letters (d, f, j, n, and p) which are used to represent only two sounds each are almost as easily made.

For a choice to be made with the d, the word must end in ed, with the d so difficult to articulate that the sound of t is substituted.

For the f, only one choice is necessary, for of is the only use of f when it does not carry its alphabet sound.

For the *j* to be sounded other than as the alphabet sound, the word is a proper noun and is supposed to be capitalized (*Navajo, San José, San Juan*).

The *p* has to be followed by *h* when the two letters spell the sound of *f* (*Philip, phone*).

The *n* has to be within a word to carry another sound. However, even within a word only one choice is needed (*thing, think, finger, wringer, anger, stranger*).

One choice is necessary for consonant blends. The combination *sc* may or may not be a blend (*scald, science, scratch, school*).

After the learners have made the transition from sight memorization through sounding the consonants, they may be taught whatever they ask about. Their interest may call for discussion of the following:

1. The letter *c*—like the *x* and the *q*—has no sound of its own but is in *cat, cents, cello, Chicago, church, Christmas, picture, musician,* and *rock*. However, *c* is silent in some words (*rock, science*), and so inner speech ignores it. In blends with *l* and *r*, the *c* uses the sound of *k* (*class, crow, scrap*) and is thereby sometimes dependable, instead of always being a nuisance.

2. A consonant blend is two or more consonant letters with no vowel letter between them.

3. Nearly all of the consonant blends may be depended upon to use the same consonant sounds in all word positions. The *sc* is the one exception. The *c* in *science* is silent.

4. The vowel sounds seem to come as if accidentally between the consonants and as a result of the same tongue and mouth movements that are needed for pronunciation of the consonant sounds.

5. The consonant letters which cause the trouble are: *c, g, h, s, t, x,* and *y*. However, the inner sound response to these letters in memorized words readily develops.

6. Learners should remember that when they encounter an unknown word, their eye focus must pass rapidly from the left

to the right as it has been doing in sentence reading. In other words, the learners must look along rapidly from the first letter to the end of the word. Readers who have made the transition from sight-memorized response to independent word recognition do this automatically. They sound through the word, listening for their inner speech to produce a word or to begin producing a word. Because they have developed the right kind and proper amount of the inner sound response to the consonant letters, they either solve the word problem immediately and continue reading or secure help.

7. The *ng* sound, using its three spellings, *ng*, *n* with *k*, and *n* with *g* (*thing*, *thingk*, *finger—fingger*). When words which are spelled in any of the three ways are learned as sight words, the inner sound response develops to the total word.

8. The letter *n*, using its alphabet sound. The *n* poses no problem when it occurs at the beginning or the end of words (*no*, *in*, *none*). However, within words it may spell its own sound (*stranger*), even with the *ng* combination, or the *ng* sound with *k* (*think*) or with *g* (*finger*).

9. At the beginning of words, *c* or *g*, capital *j*, or *s* may represent sounds other than those in their alphabet names.

10. The combination *tion* is usually sounded as if spelled *shen* (*ambition*); *cian* is sometimes *shen* (*musician*); *sion* may be sounded *zhen* (*occasion*).

11. At the end of words, *d* may be sounded *t* (*looked*, *laughed*); *t* may be used to represent the sound of *a* in *ate* (*ballet*, *bouquet*, *croquet*).

12. Letters which are "reliable" in reading may be quite the opposite for spelling. For example, the letter *k* is never any sound other than its own for reading, but the sound of *k* is spelled by *c*, *ck*, *ch*, *q*, and *k*. Five letters which are problems for reading (*d*, *h*, *n*, *p*, and *y*) will surely occur in words in which their sounds are heard. The sound of *v*, which is dependable in reading, requires an *f* in one word (*of*).*

---

* For more information, see Ellen C. Henderson, *Reading Can Be Fun*.

13. While learners are reading aloud after having read the sentence silently, they are doing the preliminary silent reading at a rapid rate and, in doing so, they are developing the important habit of seeing the known words so rapidly that the only response being practiced is the eye-mind one. In consequence, the eye-speech habit is not being overdeveloped to cause word-by-word reading and lip movement.

14. Persons who are reading aloud should realize that their purpose is to tell something, and what they say should sound like talk. They should therefore pause between phrases and look toward the listeners, but should glance at the text when they are not sure of the words instead of trying to remember.

STAGE FIVE

Preparation for Dictionary Pronunciation

Preparation for using the dictionary begins with learning the alphabet by rote. The next step is knowing the sequence of the letters.

Children can learn gradually by filing their name cards, arranging words in their word-books alphabetically, and looking for words in the picture dictionary books that are provided for pupils in the early years at school. Later they will be ready for the third step.

The third step is examination of a regular dictionary, preferably moderate-sized with a pronunciation key at the top or at the bottom of the pages. The problem is to switch the sound from the key word to the new word.

In most dictionaries there is an explanation of the key in the front of the book. The various markings (diacritical marks) seem to be complex, but they are valuable when decisions are needed, or when the new word is not in the speaking vocabulary.

Learners who can read well enough to secure meaning from a dictionary will have no problem with either vowels or consonants. They will find the pronunciation of unphonetic words immediately following the regular word.

It is possible that, except for securing the meaning, no dictionary will be needed by efficient readers who have learned to *sound rapidly through the word from the beginning to the end, correctly articulating the sounds of the phonetic consonants and ignoring the vowels, permitting the sounds of the vowels to be made as if accidentally.*

CHAPTER IV

PHONICS FOR REMEDIAL READING AND READING IMPROVEMENT CLASSES

Regardless of the reasons for which individuals are sent to remedial reading classes, phonics is fundamentally the same for all. The teacher shows the students how to make use of the sounds of the alphabet letters in acquiring the skills that are essential for efficient reading. Moreover, the procedure *at the beginning* is the same both for those who are sent and for those who come voluntarily because they are determined to improve.

The term "remedial reading" connotes finding a remedy for reading failure and implies corrective procedures.

As in all corrective situations, the causes have to be found. Learning experiences that have been omitted must be supplied. Habits which have resulted in reading failure must be replaced by habits which will result in reading success.

All of the causal factors that will be discovered stem from or merge into inability to recognize new words.

Most members of the classes will have attended school for at least two years. They usually will belong in one of the following types of classes:

1. For people who realize they are not reading efficiently.
2. For students who are not reading at their grade level.
3. For individuals who are handicapped physically or mentally or emotionally.

Only the third category is, in the strictest sense, remedial. The members require the services of specialists. Those who have poor eyesight should be fitted with glasses. Those who have a serious hearing loss should be provided with hearing aids. Those who have mental and emotional problems should be given adequate attention.

Members of this third group may be in all stages of learning to read. Some of them may be in the elementary school or in high school. Some of them may be "drop-outs." The fortunate ones may be in their first year at school, where excellent teachers are alert to channel the children for specialized services or may give the needed help as a part of the regular routine.

All remedial and improvement groups should be small and supplied with teachers who can discover the causes of failure and will supervise the activities through which reading failure will be replaced by reading success.

The steps to be taken by all members of the classes are discussed in detail in Chapter III, "Phonics."

Results will be achieved the most easily and with the least effort by the children who become members during their first or second year, for they will have fewer poor habits to overcome. However, time will be required for normal maturation.

The most rapid progress will be made by those members who have become dissatisfied with their reading habits, for they will understand explanations and be willing to follow directions. They will realize that they are becoming able to read as rapidly as they can think because they are learning to sound the consonants in a rapid left-to-right eye-mind response while they are developing the right kind and proper amount of inner speech. They will realize that they no longer have to pronounce every word or reread or read aloud in order to get the meaning. With their interest and their determination, they will achieve their goal.

The teacher's most serious problem is posed by the class members who resent being required to attend. Some of them may in their first year at school have acquired a sizable sight vocabulary but may not have made the transition from sight learning to word recognition; then later, when the word-load became too heavy for memorization, they may have had no consonant key to open the way to recognition of new words. When

they saw others reading so easily and fluently, they may have
become discouraged. Certainly they had reason to feel helpless.
The teacher's job is to show these unfortunates the consonant
short cut to reading lest they become statistics as drop-outs, D-
minus (D—) high school graduates, or delinquents.

Potential misfits are being salvaged in the remedial and
improvement classes throughout the country. For example, in
the home city of a state school for delinquents, a group of teen-
agers whose reading tests classified them as second or third
grade came into the classroom shoving each other and talking
loudly. They saw a strange teacher at the desk and their super-
intendent seated at the rear, and settled down rather defiantly
as if they dared anyone to expect anything except politeness
from them.

Within ten minutes these young people had learned that
they could sound through long words which appeared to be
difficult and were eagerly reading an interesting article in the
local newspaper.

The young people knew much more than had been meas-
ured by the conventional intelligence test, or they would not
have been able to begin to read so quickly. Some of them may
have acquired a "sight" vocabulary during their first school
experiences but have failed to be successful enough to enjoy
their reading. They may not have realized that their disinterest
in school stemmed from inability to read, or that simple mischief
in the schoolroom would grow into offenses serious enough to
send them to a reformatory.

A twelfth-year student who had received "social" promo-
tions each year was being graduated from high school with an
above-average grade because he had been able to answer
examination and test questions orally after hearing the class dis-
cussions and listening to his mother as she read his lessons. He
had figured his mathematical problems and signed his name to
the papers. Yet neither he nor his mother nor his teachers realized that if he could read numbers and his name, he could learn
to read print.

The young man covered all of the essential steps that he

had missed. He followed all of the directions and made as many repetitions as the reading specialist suggested. Owing to his never having developed exaggerated inner speech, he had no word-by-word habits with which to cope, and was able, from the first lesson, to read silently as rapidly as he was thinking.

Reading failure is no proof of a low intelligence quotient (IQ), although it may be interpreted as such. A youngster in his seventh year at school shared the belief of his teachers that children with his family name could not learn. Because he had no inclination to create any disturbance, day after day for six years he sat quietly. He listened to everything that was said and looked at the text when others were reading aloud. The teachers said that he was a sweet child. They had him run errands and clean the erasers.

A teacher took the boy to a university class where a reading specialist was demonstrating a system of phonics. The boy watched as the instructor had some little children point to and name the alphabet letters, then some older children memorize and read aloud some sentences which they had dictated for her to print on the chalkboard, and still older children tell about how the letters of which words are made have sounds as well as names. The instructor said she would hear the oldest children read and would tell them the words which they did not at once recognize. The boy was asked to read. He looked at the first word, then looked toward the instructor. She told him the word and added, "I'll tell you how I can find out what a new word is. I look along the letters and I can hear myself think the sounds of a word I already have used in my talk. Then if I want to, I'll say the word. Of course, I can see more than one word while I'm looking. But you may say just one word. Go ahead now, and try to read."

The boy said, "I can't read the way you're reading, but I can think the words to myself when I'm looking at them."

The instructor said, "When you are thinking the words at which you are looking, you are really reading. That is fine. However, this paper from your school tells me that you have never read at all. Why didn't you read in your classroom?"

"The teachers never asked me to read," the boy answered.

"Why didn't you read when it came your turn to read?"

"They didn't wait for me to begin, and someone else read instead."

The instructor asked, "Did you offer to read, ever?"

"Once or twice I did, a long time ago. The teachers made me put my hand down. I didn't care; because if I couldn't read, I just couldn't."

The instructor said, "We'd like to hear you read to us, now. However, first please point to the letters of the alphabet and say the name of each one."

The boy named the letters. He then began pronouncing the words in the book from which the oldest children had read aloud.

When he hesitated, the instructor showed him how to go through the word rapidly, sounding only the consonants.

The instructor said, "I'm going to tell the men and women in this big class what I think are the reasons for your being able to say the words to yourself. Your teacher will talk with you later and answer any questions you may want to ask.

"Owing to the experience this boy has had with the alphabet letters, his inner sound response was developed to the twenty-three letters which carry one of their sounds in their alphabet names; and later, while he was looking at the words which others were speaking in their reading aloud, his inner speech was developing to other phonetic elements and to 'sight' words."

The instructor asked the boy if he would like her to show him how to read aloud so well that everybody would enjoy listening to him. She then showed him how to sound new words silently before beginning to read a sentence or phrase, and how to do the preliminary silent reading rapidly without pronouncing each word.

Discouraged members of remedial classes should believe that it is possible for them to learn to read.

In a school system of a big city, the members of several forty-minute reading "improvement" classes were pupils who had attended school seven years but were unable to pass a third-year reading test. The teacher became ill. The substitute teacher who was provided was given permission to experiment during the absence of the regular teacher.

The new teacher spent her first day observing while the regular teacher was present. She also selected sets of test papers and copied some of the reading scores.

Next day she said to each class: "I'm to be your teacher for a few days. I have here some informal tests which your teacher gave you a few weeks ago. The scores are rather low. I'm sure you don't like poor marks. Of course, when the marks are poor, it is because the answers were not right, for if the answers are right the scores will be high.

"There are tricks to answering questions. If you would like to earn some high scores, I can show you some of the tricks.

"In a test no one is going to tell you the words, so you must be able to know them without being told. I can show you how to do that.

"You have to be sure about what the question is asking you to do. Under this map I've printed one of the test questions. When I uncover the question, begin to read. If you come to a word you don't know, let me tell you the word. Now I'll uncover the question.

"I'll cover the question again, because no one asked me to tell any words. There is a word in the sentence that some of you didn't know when you took the test because some of you drew lines under words instead of making rings around them. I'll draw a ring around the word I'm talking about. Please don't even whisper it if you know it (*circle*), because those who don't know it should have a chance to learn it themselves.

"I know the word partly because I know that a *c* at the beginning of a word may use the sound of *s* and a *c* in the middle of a word sometimes uses the sound of *k*. I'll print the word as it sounds: *sirkle*. The sound of *s* is in the name of the *s*. The sound of the *k* is in the name of the *k*. Say the sounds with me while I keep the chalk under the sounds which we'll be making. I'll move the chalk slowly between the *s* and the *r*. But I'll move it quickly from the *r* to the *k* and the *l*. Then say the word.

"Of course, you know the word is *circle*. *Circle* is a synonym of *ring*.

"If the word in the question had been *ring* instead of *circle*, the score on the question might have been high. Now it is zero.

"On this other test paper, there are rings around some of the words, but the pupil either didn't know the meaning of *synonym* or he doesn't know some of the words, because his score is zero.

"Your scores depend upon whether you know the meaning, but if you can pronounce the words correctly, you are likely to remember their meaning because you have heard others use them in talking and you may have been told them in your reading classes at some other time. So the trick I'll show you now is how to sound through a word.

"You know that all the words in the dictionary are made up from the twenty-six letters of the alphabet. There are two kinds of letters, vowels and consonants. There is a vowel in every word and every part of words which have more than one syllable, and there is at least one consonant in all words except two, *I* and a little word spelled with the first letter of the alphabet (*a*) but pronounced like the first letter of *alone*.

"I'll put the consonants of a word which you know on the chalkboard. When you see just its consonant letters, you will remember the word. Don't say the word, just think it and hold up your hand so I'll see that you know it.

"I'll now print the consonants of a word without its vowel letters.

"Look at this skeleton word (*r—m—mb—r*). Let's sound through it. You know the word.

"I'll put a few more skeleton words on the chalkboard and we'll sound through all of them."

v—w—l   w—rk   r—v—r   st—nd
t—l—ph—ne   sk—l—t—n

The teacher said, "What you are doing, boys and girls, is sounding the consonant letters. The vowel sounds come in between the consonant sounds. You hear yourself say a word. If you have heard the word before and have known its meaning, you remember it. If you are reading, the word which is in your mind should fit into the meaning of the sentence.

"We have only twenty-six letters but we have forty definite sounds; so that some of the letters are used for more than one sound. In *circle* the letter *c* is used to represent two different sounds. The letter *c* helps to spell other sounds, too. Later I'll show them to you.

"But right now, I'll show you one of the best tricks of all.

"Say the letters of the alphabet while I print them across the board from left to right."

a	b			c
		d		
e		f		g
			h	
i		j		
	k			
	l			
	m	n		
o		p		
	q			
	r			s
				t
u	v			
	w			x
				y
	z			

"I'll print five words in consonant skeleton form:

r—m—mb—r v—w—l z—r— w—rk qu—ll

"One by one, please come and select a letter of a word, then draw a circle around the same letter in the alphabet letters.

"All of the letters in the skeleton words are either vowels or else are in the first column of consonants. This is one of the promised tricks, for whenever you see any of the nine conso-

nant letters, you can use the sound in recognizing the unknown
or forgotten word. Of course, you must make the sounds correctly.

"Five other letters are almost as useful as the nine. I'll tell
you about them later. You can see the other five in the third
column.

"Today, read these test questions to find the words you
need to know in order to pass with a high score.

"Here are fresh copies of the test. Before you begin writing
the answers, read all of the questions. Hold up your hand if you
come to a word you don't know, and I'll help you."

The young people in these groups became so enthusiastic
that they surprised all of their teachers by earning promotion to
the eighth grade.

Many of the pupils in the groups were unable to say the
alphabet without either omitting or misplacing some of the
letters. Not one of them could make all of the consonant sounds.
They had to learn how to make some of them without adding
a vowel. In sounding the consonants, their inner speech imitated
their oral pronunciation, and they heard *teree* instead of *tree,
guhooduh* instead of *good, buhuhlackuh* instead of *black,* and
so on. In consequence, they had much to learn.

However, they were strongly motivated. They were determined to learn what the teacher was willing to teach.

In a few days they worked through the essentials of learning to read and were soon able to recognize most of the words
in books which were meant for good readers in the fourth grade.
They were bringing articles from newspapers and magazines
to read aloud in the class. In oral reading they imitated the
teacher's interpretation of humorous selections and thereby were
learning to read in phrases with pauses between the phrases.
Most important of all, they were developing a rapid rate of
silent reading, for they had to read the oncoming phrase silently
before they could read it aloud. In this way they were overcoming the word-by-word habit they had been handicapped
with all during their school life.

Anyone who wishes to break himself of his poor reading habits can do so. He must first realize that his eyes can see words much more rapidly than his speech muscles can produce them, and that he can become able to read as rapidly as he wishes to think about the subject matter with which he is to deal. Then he must give himself the learning experience through which his sight-mind association will become stronger than his sight-speech association.

Replacement of slow sight-speech habits may be accomplished in two ways.

One way is for the reader deliberately to force *his eyes and his mind* to deal with ideas instead of with word units. To accomplish this, he must make it impossible for his speech muscles to pronounce the words while his eyes see them.

He should provide himself with a clock or watch and a device such as a ruler or piece of cardboard to aid in control of the left-to-right focusing of the eyes, for he must make no regressive trips to check for probable inaccuracies. Moreover, if he finds that his eyes have a tendency to look away from the print, he should look at each sentence through a slit which has been cut just wide enough for a line of print to show through.

The first reading should be of interesting content in which none of the words is difficult. Until after he has given himself a few training experiences, the sentences should be short, preferably no more than one line in length.

Fortified with unlimited determination and the firm intention to concentrate all of his attention upon the matter in hand, he should record the time and begin to read. Should he be distracted by anything whatsoever, he should at once stop reading and record the time.

From the number of words he has read in a given time he can know whether his rate is improving.

Another way is to read aloud, because in order to read effectively, it is necessary to read silently in advance of the voice. This silent reading may be done at a spectacularly rapid rate. In a quick glance the eyes can see along a wide field, provided that the words are familiar. Of course, the rate will be reduced momentarily if there is a new word in the oncoming phrase. However, inner speech will immediately deal with the unfamiliar word before the reader speaks the first word of the phrase, and the silent-then-oral reading continues.

An excellent self-checking device for the individual who is using the oral-reading route toward rapid reading, is to read before a mirror with himself as his audience. He should look at the text only while he is securing the meaning of the oncoming phrases, then toward himself while he talks. In this way he is forcing his eyes and his mind to disregard the established habits of sight-speech. Moreover, he is proving that he can do silent reading while he is pausing between the phrases and at the end of sentences. His next step is to use the rapid reading skills at all times except when he chooses to read slowly.

The oral-reading road to rapid silent reading is particularly good because an effective oral reader does not lose his rapid reading habits even while he is reading slowly. In his inner speech he reads to himself in much the same way that he reads to himself at the mirror. His inner speech reflects his oral reading habits and he actually skips and skims over the words. A photographic record of his eye movements would show the usual number of fixations upon the words, but many of the fixations would be bunched together at the spots where he did his collateral thinking. The bunches of fixations representing his collateral thoughts also represent time that is well spent. It takes time to enjoy the rhythm of poetry and prose, to enjoy the music of words strung together in beauty or in truth, to live vicariously through the experiences of others, and to hope from their mistakes to avoid some on our own part.

Steps for remedial phonics

Be sure that the learners realize that reading is *understanding* the meaning, and that all of the words in the language are made of just the twenty-six letters of the alphabet.

1. Put the figure 26 in the upper right-hand corner of a sheet of paper (or the chalkboard).

2. Ask the learners to say the letters while you print them across from left to right (as they appear on an earlier page).*

3. Ask to be told that the five letters at the left of the sheet are vowels. Draw a perpendicular line down at the left of the five.

4. Subtract 5 from 26 and remark that the twenty-one letters remaining after the subtraction are the other kind of letters, the consonants.

5. Print "*v o w e l*" and lead the learners in making the sounds of the letters.

6. Hold your pencil (or chalk) under each consonant while you and they make the three consonant sounds; but after making the sound of *v*, move the pencil rapidly across the *o* to the *w*, then move it rapidly across the *e* to the *l*.

7. Repeat this a few times.

8. Print the consonants with a dash (−) replacing each vowel:

v−w−l

9. Lead the learners in making the sounds of the letters.

10. Explain that all of the vowel sounds that are in words are made while the breath is coming through the mouth, and therefore the dashes are a signal for the learner to open his jaws so that the vowel sound will come out.

11. Repeat as in Numbers 6 and 9. (Be sure to make the sounds of *v* and *w* correctly, and also to skip rapidly across the dashes which are representing the *o* and the *e*.)

12. Ask the learners to listen to hear *vowel* in their minds, their inner speech.

13. Remark that you must be sure they know what you mean by *inner speech*, and that you will give them two numbers for them to add and tell you the answer.

---

* See p. 87.

14. Say "Five and five" (or "Two and two"). They will give the answer.

15. Hold your hand (pencil or chalk) upward and say that you will give two more numbers but they are not to give the answer until your hand goes down. Do so.

16. Remind the learners that the answer they thought *in their minds* is inner speech.

17. Say, "I'll print some words that you know." Print: *run, red, bell, mud.* Say, "You remember how I put a dash for the vowel letter. Now I'll print the words with a dash instead of each vowel.

red	run	bell	mud
r–d	r–n	b–ll	m–d

"Remember to open your jaws when you see a vowel letter inside a word or at its beginning. (The *e* at the end of some words does not use a sound; it is silent.)"

18. Do with the four words as you did with *v__w__l.*

19. Say (*a*) that you will now print a skeleton of another word, (*b*) that they will hear what they have heard you say, and (*c*) that you think they will be able to know what the word is if they sound through it as they sounded *vowel, red, bell, mud,* and *run.*

20. Print: *r–m–mb–r.* Ask for lifted hands if they know the word. (If anyone doesn't lift his hand, have him come to you and—with your help, if necessary—recognize the word.)

21. To give the learners a second successful experience, print:

n–mb–r

22. Show on the alphabetical scheme that the six consonants in *vowel* and *remember* are in the first column of consonants, and say, "Whenever you see any of these nine consonants in a word, you can use its sound and in your inner speech you can hear a word. If the word you hear fits into the meaning of the sentence you are reading, you can go on reading."

23. Give each student a sheet of sentences which are made

of words using the nine letters. (Several sentences are on page 50.)

24. Say, "You need to know something about five other letters. They are in the second column of consonant letters on the alphabetical scheme. The five are *d, f, j, n,* and *p.*"

25. The *d* never uses more than two sounds, as in *red* and *looked.*

26. The *f* is the sound of *f* in every word except *of,* where it is *v.*

27. The *j* is the sound of *j* except in a few words from foreign languages, as *San Juan, José, Navajo.*

28. The *n* is always the *n* sound at the beginning and at the end of words, but within many words it spells or helps to spell the two-letter *ng* sound (*sing, finger, ink*).

29. Say, "When the *p* is not followed by *h* (*telephone, phone*), it is the sound of *p,* so that the *p* is a fifth letter which never is used for more than two sounds."

30. The nine one-sound letters and the five two-sound letters make fourteen sounds that are useful in recognizing new words. The other seven consonants (*h, c, g, s, t, x, y*) cause most of the trouble. However, when two or more consonants come together without a vowel sound in between, the consonants blend together and inner speech sounds a word. Say, "You have to watch out for one consonant blend, the *sc.* In *scald* the *sc* is a blend, but in *science* the *c* is silent."

31. In consonant blends with *l* and *r* the *c* is the sound of *k* and the *g* is the sound of *g* in *go.* The *t* is the sound of *t* in all blends. Moreover, excepting *sc,* the *s* is its *s* sound in blends.

32. Thus only *h* and *x* and *y* are really troublesome.

33. The *h* is its *h* sound (just breath) at the beginning of words, but it helps to spell the two-letter sounds which are at the beginning of these words: *Chicago, Christmas, church, phone, she, this, think,* and *where.* However, excepting *ch,* the two-letter sounds are very useful in learning new words because inner speech becomes accustomed to using them. Inner speech uses even *ch* easily.

34. Inner speech seems to ignore silent letters. We may try

to pronounce them, but we find it difficult. We don't try to pronounce the *k* and *w* of *know,* the *gh* of *light* and *through,* the *l*
of *walk,* the *p* of *pneumonia,* or the like.

35. Inner speech seems to ignore the vowel letters. The
reason it can do so is this: the vowel sounds are vibrating breath
which are what they are because of changes in the mouth cavity
while the vibrating, vocal breath is emerging. The changes in
shape are brought about by the movements which are made in
order to produce the twenty-five consonant sounds. The movements are made by the lips, the tongue, the soft palate, and the
jaws.

CHAPTER V

ESSENTIALS OF READING FOR BEGINNERS

Despite what has been said and written about reading methods, reading skills and abilities, and reading failure, the process of learning to read has always been what it now is. A learner is curious about the words or the letters he sees. Either directly or indirectly he asks to be told about a word or a letter or a group of words. While he is looking at the text, he hears an answer. At that instant an invisible something happens between the eye machinery and the thinking apparatus, and he remembers a part or all of what he has been told. When his eyes again focus on the text, the invisible something may again occur. If he speaks the words while he is looking at them, the speech apparatus is included in the process.

When his eyes are focused on the words while he is speaking them, the inner sound response is developing. He can think the meaning and speak the words. He can organize the new meaning into the ideas which he already has. In this recognition of meaning and organization of it, he is reading.

Many individuals learn so easily and quickly and with so little help that they are reading long before they are aware of it. Many children are reading before they are old enough to attend school. Teachers and parents know this. Most teachers of first grade find that within a few weeks of the beginning of school, some of the children are reading first-grade-level material fluently and accurately.

However, data show that these children had early experience with the alphabet letters, such as playing with ABC blocks, talking about words or letters on television or in newspapers or magazines, cutting out letters, printing their names, and so on.

But unless these rapid learners—children, teenagers, or adults—had a severe hearing loss or defective eyesight, they were using the sounds of the alphabet of the language, for individuals everywhere learn to read and spell by mastering the sound-symbols of their language, whatever the symbols happen to be.

Although we think of reading as "knowing the meaning of words," the term "reading" has more than one connotation. A dictionary of almost any size makes such statements as these:

> Reading is getting information or amusement from written or printed symbols.
> Reading may mean a public recital where something is read to the audience.
> Reading may mean the written or printed words to be read, as, "There is little reading in this picture magazine."
> Reading may mean a kind of reading material; we take a monthly reading of an instrument.

Kinds of reading. Much has been written and said about the "kinds" of reading, oral and silent. As a matter of fact, there are many kinds of reading: skipping, scanning, reading aloud, and so on. But all reading is first of all a silent process, a mental contact between a symbol and its meaning. For people who can see, sight is the means of contact.

For people who can see to be able to know the meaning of words as a result of looking at them is quite as miraculous as for the blind individual to be reading while his fingers are moving along the tiny raised surfaces of paper. When we realize how the blind read, we are amazed at the complexity of the reading process. We might with consistency be amazed to realize that something equally complex is happening while an individual who can see is reading, for he is securing the meaning because of a pulsating movement which is within the eye. Securing the meaning through this inner activity is as miraculous as securing meaning through the sense of touch.

During reading, this pulsating movement is as continuous

as the heartbeat. We can get some idea of this movement if we observe closely while we tap the point of a pin on a hard surface. We realize that for an instant between tappings, the point of the pin is at rest. There is just such an interval of rest between the eye pulsations. It is during the intervals of rest that sight occurs. Indeed, during the intervals of motion there is no sight at all. If the pulsations were slow enough, we would be blind part of the time. We are able to see because the pulsations are so rapid that they merge. As a result of the merging we have what seems to be continuous vision.

We have moving pictures because somebody made use of what had been discovered about eye movement and found a way to set hundreds of pictures revolving so that they merge to give continuous vision. At the turn of the present century, people could look through a peephole and see a ball game or a prizefight.

Thomas A. Edison made use of what was known about eye movement and invented the kinetoscope; and apparatus was devised to take photographs of eye movement during reading. For nearly fifty years people have been able to study photographic records. Early investigators proved that we are reading while the eye movement is momentarily fixed. They called the "fixed" period—the period of rest—a fixation pause. They called the amount which the eye can see during a fixation pause the "field of vision." They demonstrated that during the instant of fixation the eyes can see across a wide field of vision provided the mind is doing its part in interpreting the meaning of the words which the eye can see.

One of the significant things that were learned from the early study of photographs of eye movement was that people who were reading at a slow rate were pronouncing the words either in a whisper or with definite movement of the speech muscles. The conclusion was that people who read slowly are probably thinking slowly at their talking rate, or perhaps reading with divided attention. Tests indicated that slow readers were likely to forget the first part of the sentence before they had reached the end. The eye-movement photographs showed that slow readers frequently had to go back to the first part of the sentence and reread. It seemed evident that those readers who secured the meaning in the least time were able quickly to make use of the ideas in a way that was an advantage in remembering what had been read. In fact, the indications were that the fastest readers retained more of what they read than was retained by the people who read at a slower rate.

People who read rapidly may have as few as two fixations on a four- or five-inch-long line of print. It is possible for a reader to have only one fixation per line. This could happen when someone is reading aloud from a partially or completely memorized text. The reader glances at the text, as if to be absolutely sure about the words he is about to speak. In that glance he may seem to read the entire line. However, a photograph of the eye movement would probably show only one fixation and that single fixation might be located at any point along the line or even below or above it.

Actually, the sight of one or more words may have touched off the miraculous eye-brain power from which reading stems, wherein at the sight of clue words the remainder of the meaning pops into the mind. This type of reading is more memorization than real interpretation of the printed page. Such spectacularly rapid reading may be done by people whose work or hobby calls for an enormous amount of daily reading.

Learning to read

The paragraphs which follow are essential to all individuals of any age who are having their first learning-to-read experience.

1. Learners should realize that reading is a silent process, that it is a mental contact in which the eyes see the reading symbols and the mind thinks the meaning, organizing the new idea with the ideas which already are in the mind of the reader.

2. The learner must be able to point to and name the letters of the alphabet. This is important. Beginners should early use the letters as clues in distinguishing between words which look

alike or are used in the same way. For example, with two sentences which have the same general context (*This is my name/ Here is my name*), someone can say, "I know this word is *here* because *here* has an *h*," or "*This* begins with *th*." Furthermore, learners who can point to and name the alphabet letters have already developed the automatic sound response to twenty-three of the twenty-six letters, fourteen of which are reliable in the sense that when the eyes focus on them in definite word positions their sounds may be used without question in word recognition.

3. The learner should be making all of the consonant sounds correctly. If the consonant sounds are made correctly, the vowel values in the words are likely to be satisfactorily produced in between the consonants and thereby are ably cooperating in the inner speech process.

4. The learner should be speaking with flexible jaw movement, thereby making it possible for good vowel production; for all of the definite vowel sounds are produced as a result of changes in the shape of the mouth cavity, and flexible jaw movement is an important factor. Children whose first speech is "baby talk" probably have been unable to see the tip-of-tongue movement which results in the two *th* sounds (*this, thin*) or the rising of the tongue which is a part of the sound of *r*. Tight jaw movement of others in the environment is a handicap to children who are learning to talk.

5. Individuals who can see should master two new habits neither of which was being practiced before in connection with learning to read. The two new habits are *thinking the meaning of the words while the eyes are focused on them,* and *focusing the eyes on the words in a rapid movement from left to right.*

Neither of the new habits "comes naturally." It is no more natural for the English language to be read from the left to the right than it is for other languages to be read in other directions. Indeed, the natural thing to do is to focus the eyes in any or all directions as the eyes behave when we look at any flat surface such as a picture—or a word—whether we are merely looking or are concerned about the significances that may be attached to the flat surface—or the word. Mere pronunciation is not reading. Reading is knowing the meaning. An infant can see *mamma* and say "Mamma," but is that reading? Fortunately, the infant's eyes do not remain focused on the word long enough to develop a permanent habit.

Beginners must also practice a third habit, *removal of the focus from the words*. This is accomplished automatically while the left-to-right habit is operating. This looking away is unconsciously practiced by children when they point to a letter or word and ask to be told what it is or "says." They probably continue to look while they are hearing the answer. They may say the word at least once, but they are likely to look away immediately.

The importance of the three habits should not be underestimated. No one knows how many individuals have failed to learn to read because no one discovered that they did not *at the right time* learn to look from left to right along the line of print. No one knows how many children and adults read slowly word by word because they did not learn to *think the meaning at the instant their eyes were focused on the words and instantly look forward along the line or otherwise remove the eye focus from the word*.

The three habits may be learned in sentences which have the same words at the beginning but different words toward the end.

6. Beginners should also learn words by the direct route between the sight of the word and its meaning. For example, to learn *book*, they should see the printed word and a book at the same time. The learner's speech machine has been producing the spoken word and the meaning is in his mind. When his eyes focus on both the book and the printed word, that invisible something begins to occur between what he sees and what he thinks. A two-way association begins between the sight-word and the mind-word. If he pronounces the word, his speech machine gets into the associative process to begin a three-way association (sight-mind-speech). This sight-mind-speech association is an essential step. However, it is useful only in learning situations

in which the reader encounters an unknown word. It is the sight-mind response upon which the reading process is based, for reading is first of all a silent response.

Words which are the names of things are easily learned in the sight-meaning way. The printed form of a word which is filed in the learner's brain is put on or next to an object, for example, a chair. The eyes are kept focused for an instant on *chair* while the learner thinks *"chair."* A mental picture of the word is stamped in the brain. If the learner listens, he can hear an inner pronunciation of the word. This inner response is useful for word recognition. However, it is also the cause of slow, inefficient, word-by-word silent and oral reading. *The eyes must not remain focused on the words.* While the eyes remain focused on the words, inner pronunciation continues to clamor for the position of supremacy it has held ever since the learner first spoke the word; and in order to keep the very essential inner response where it belongs, the learner must remove his eye focus to some other locality and do his thinking and talking about *chair* without pronouncing it while his eyes are focused on the word.

The word *chair* is an excellent example because in almost any room there will be at least two chairs, probably of different size or make. This being the case, the learner can see the same word in different locations. The teacher can add to the learning experience by having the word printed in different sizes and kinds of letters and on several colors and sizes of paper, thus making sure that the learners are seeing the word itself instead of the environment.

Sentences with the same words at the beginning but different words at the end may be substituted for the usual "experience" sentences which many teachers use to help the beginners find out how much they are to benefit from being able to read.

The adults readily understand about the necessity for making numerous repetitions in order to learn the new habit. They can consciously move their eyes along the lines from left to right. But children require others to make decisions for them. However, the content of the sentences should be interesting to them. The solution is to have the children dictate the sentences. The teacher can choose the sentence form. After a trip to the store or a walk to the park, the children would probably be satisfied with the following:

> We went for a walk today.
> We saw a little dog.
> We saw a little cat.
> We saw a little girl.
> We saw a little boy.

The following type of sentence is offered in a book for adults who are having their first learning-to-read experiences:

> We have to know that the sound of this *c* is *k*.
> We have to know that the sound of this *c* is *s*.
> We have to know that the sound of this *s* is *z*.
> We have to know that the sound of this *wh* is *hw*.*

7. Beginners of any age should develop the automatic sound response to the letters which spell the two-letter sounds before they see them in the words of which they will name the letters. For this reason the experience sentences should use words beginning with *wh, th, sh, ph,* and *ch* before the initial letters are used in words. Because *ch* is used in three spellings (*school, Chicago, church*), the *ch* sound should not be discussed. The words should be treated merely as sight words.

The following sentences discuss the two-letter sounds in the order they are presented in the section of the book dealing with procedures in the first grade:

> This is my name: _____.

With this sentence there will begin developing the inner sound response to the four words (*is, my, name,* and *this*), to the voiced *th,* and to *s* in the final word position as the sound of both *s* and *z*.

---

* Ellen C. Henderson and Twila L. Henderson, *Learning to Read and Write* (New York: Holt, Rinehart and Winston, 1965).

What is your name?

In this sentence the eyes' focus is on the *wh* but the inner pronunciation develops according to the speech form, with the sound of *h* preceding the sound of *w*. Thus there will be developed the inner response to both the *h* and the *w*. Inner response will also be developed to the initial *y*, the third letter to which no automatic sound response was developed while the alphabet was being learned. Moreover, two new words (*what* and *your*) become "sight" words.

Where is the phone? Where is your phone?
Where is Phoebe? Phyllis?

In the sentences above, the *ph* releases the *p* for later sentences and sight words.

Three books are in this room.
Do you think there are three books in this room?

The sentences take care of the breathy *th*.

Where is Mary? She is in the other room.
Is Mary in the other room? Yes, she is in the other room.

In the above sentences, the sight words present the *y* in two different word positions. If some alert adult asks a question about the two uses, he might be shown a third word position of *y* ("Mary will try").

Will the bell ring? Yes, the bell will ring.

These sentences release the *ng* sound. Later the initial *g* will be available in its initial word position representing the sound of *g* that is in *go*.

Will James go to church? Yes, James will go to church.

The *ch* paves the way for the other two uses of the *ch* combination, as in the following:

Will Amos go to school? Yes, Amos will go to school.
Will Joseph go to Chicago? Yes, Joseph will go to Chicago.

8. Beginners should memorize the sentences by a direct route between the sight of the string of words and the meaning. The teacher supplies the meaning, and the members of the class let their eyes look from the first familiar words to the new word at the end.

The learners must realize that words are made of alphabet letters. Adults already understand this, and very young children readily comprehend that the letters in words are exactly like the alphabet letters.

9. The learners should discover that letters have sounds. They might make the discovery as a result of the teacher's questions about mouth movements that are easily seen and felt while the sound is being made, coupled with an explanation which would include the remainder of the sounds in the word being used as a demonstration.

10. The learners should look at the words only long enough for their eyes and their minds to secure the meaning. As soon as they have secured a mental image of the words, they should look away either to read aloud or to make additional repetitions of what they have just seen and thought.

11. Beginners should willingly tell the teacher and others what they have read. This telling others actually is reading aloud.

The oral reading may be done in group response with all members of the group speaking spontaneously and no one waiting for someone else to begin speaking.

Always, before speaking the first word of a sentence, the readers should glance along the string of words to read silently before reading aloud. The preliminary glance will constitute an exceptionally rapid silent response.

12. Beginners who read aloud should look away from the text while they "talk the ideas." This is important. In the first place, in looking away from the text they are practicing the third of the three habits that were learned at the beginning of the learning-to-read experiences, thereby avoiding overdevelopment of inner pronunciation. In the second place, they never will learn to read word by word, either silently or aloud. In the

third place, they will be reading silently at a rapid rate, for before they read aloud they look rapidly along the sentence that they are about to "tell to someone." In the fourth place, when the motive is to tell something, the voice will behave exactly as it does during conversation, and the oral reading will be effective because it will sound like talk. (See *Reading Can Be Fun,* by Henderson.)

13. All reading aloud should be phrased as people talk, with pauses between the phrases. A spoken phrase is a unit idea. It may be one word or it may be an entire sentence. The following sentences are printed in phrases:

> I am going to the exhibit
> in the morning.
>
> Father went to the church
> to listen to the sermon.
>
> The monkeys
> jump from tree to tree.
>
> The zebra will be with the lion
> or the tiger.
>
> David looked in the room
> and locked the door.

14. Learners should be able to know what they have accomplished. Children can have word-books, lists of words, or pages of sentences they have memorized or are learning to read. Older learners can make use of checking devices and conferences.

15. Learners should ask for help when they fail to understand what is being taught or when they have forgotten. They will be the more likely to request help if they can feel sure that a minimum of attention or embarrassment will be attached to their request or to the answer.

16. The teacher should explain inner speech. The beginners have been making use of it. The adults will experience no difficulty and can use the term if they choose to do so; and the young people, after they begin to talk about sounds and sound-

ing, can understand that they know the answer of a problem such as that five and five are ten and can hear the answer in their minds before they say "Ten". After they use the term a few times, it will cease being abstract.

The teacher should explain that phonics is the use which is made of the sounds of the alphabet letters; that phonics is based on inner speech; and that the consonant letters hold the key to effective phonics. To children "phonics" is an abstract term, much less useful than simple explanations about how the words are made up of the sounds of letters. Consonant phonics uses no vowel rules to puzzle people with exceptions.

17. The students should see words with silent letters listed on the chalkboard or on the bulletin board with the letters which are silent matched with the same silent letter in other words, as in the following lists:

know	light	laugh	walk	thumb
knew	thought	laughed	talk	lamb
write	enough	enough	chalk	

18. The learners should pronounce the indefinite article *a* correctly. The little word should never be given the sound of the first alphabet letter except when it is in a position of emphasis, as it is in the first sentence of this paragraph. Any speaker—or reader—who mispronounces it is merely carrying on an incorrect habit which someone permitted him to learn.

19. The teacher should be sure that the learners understand that reading is securing the meaning, not mere calling words. Even when the learners are reading down columns of words, the meaning of every word should be known to the reader. While the learners are looking at lists of words, they should *look to be sure of the word, then look away to pronounce it*. It should be remembered that the eye continues its inner pulsations while focused on the word and thereby is continuing to develop too much automatic sound response.

20. Mature readers should realize that inner speech is an advantage when the reader encounters an unknown word, but when it is overdeveloped it compels the reader to frame each

word, sometimes in a whisper and sometimes aloud. Such word-by-word reading limits the rate of reading to the rate of his oral pronunciation, a rate which is far slower than efficient reading needs to be.

To be compelled to read as slowly as one pronounces is a serious handicap, unless, of course, the reader has to practically memorize what he is reading. An efficient reader can choose his reading rate and thereby read to enjoy poetry or well-written prose, or read slowly for some other good reason.

21. Learners should realize that they do not have to remain in the grip of inefficient habits with their eyes focused on the words as they pronounce each one. They should be taught how to develop this miraculous inner-speech power by training their eye focus to pass rapidly toward the next printed unit while their minds interpret the meaning as rapidly as they are able to think. Then the only time when the inner-speech response will be operating is when the reader encounters an unknown word or has some other good reason for making use of it.

* * *

Learning to read would be much simplified if changes were to be made in the spelling of some of the unphonetic words. The word *of* is the only one to use *f* when it does not represent its own sound. The *j* represents its own sound except in proper nouns such as *San Juan* and *San José*. The *p* would be phonetic if words which use *ph* were to be spelled with *f*. Then if silent letters were eliminated, four letters (*b, k, l,* and *w,* as in *thumb, know, talk,* and *answer*) would be perfectly coded in all words. If *t* were added at the end of words spelled with *ed* but pronounced with *t*, thirteen of the alphabet letters would be completely phonetic. Instead of being faced with unphonetic words (*know, write, telephone, sleigh, laughed, through, should, shoulder,* and so on), learners would have more words to be recognized or remembered through the simple process of sounding.

CHAPTER VI

PHONICS IN THE FIRST GRADE

This chapter describes what was attempted in two first grades by teachers who were guided by the author while they were trying out the phonics activity that is discussed in this book. Both teachers had taught either in the second grade or the junior high school. Neither had taught in the first grade, but both had taught pupils who were failing because they could not read at their grade level.

At the beginning of the school year, the children were examined for health, vision, and hearing. All of them had spent one year attending half-day sessions in kindergarten.

During the first week of September they were given a review of the alphabet. They said the alphabet by rote while they were looking at the letters and could hear them pronounced. They were then asked to bring to the teacher all they "knew" of the letters which were available on tables in the room. The letters were of various sizes and colors, and printed in both upper and lower case. Some of them were clipped from newspapers and magazines. Some of them were hand-printed.

Each child brought letters but most of them were duplicates. No child could name more than three of the letters he brought to the desk.

In meetings with the two teachers who would be using the proposed system of consonant phonics, the following concepts were accepted.

Reading is a meaningful response to printed or written symbols. It is a silent activity resulting from association between the muscles which control sight and thought.

During oral reading an additional response brings into

action the muscles which control speech. Thus, whereas reading is a sight-meaning response, oral reading is a sight-meaning-speech response.

It is possible for the sight-meaning-speech response to become merely sight-speech, whereby the reader can pronounce the words without thinking the meaning. *Catkick*, a meaningless combination of letters, is easily spoken.

This sight-speech power is highly important. Through it the reader can make use of the sounds of the alphabet letters in word recognition. The reader focuses his eyes on a letter—or a combination of letters—and if his eye focus passes rapidly along the word from left to right, *and if he has learned to make the consonant sounds correctly,* he can hear a word in his inner speech. If the word he hears fits into the meaning of the sentence, the sight-meaning response can take over and he can continue at his habitual rate of reading.

All of the children must be "ready" physically, mentally, and emotionally. Experiences, either in the home or the kindergarten or during the first weeks of the first year, should include the following:

1. Asking questions and receiving answers.
2. Being able to respond when spoken to.
3. Being able to sit relaxed while listening to someone.
4. Listening to someone who is reading to him.
5. Memorizing Mother Goose and related rhymes.
6. Looking at books, pictures, magazines, television, and so forth.
7. Looking at books and pretending to read.
8. Telling about something that has happened, a story.
9. Speaking with no incorrect sounds (baby talk).
10. Using terms of politeness (*thank you, please,* and so forth).
11. Talking about what they see in stores, parks, and so on.
12. Speaking in sentences. (One word may have sentence meaning.)
13. Talking about the shape of things (*round, square, pointed*).
14. Telling the colors of things.

15. Talking about differences and likenesses.
16. Being able to follow directions.
17. Knowing some of the common signs (STOP, WALK, and so on).
18. Being able to point to and name the alphabet letters.
19. Printing names—their own and those of others.
20. Counting while pointing or touching things.

The two teachers accepted the plan to guide the children through four stages of development: readiness, sight memorization, transition from sight learning to independent word recognition, and independent word recognition.

In addition to the usual first grade supplies, the teachers had access to printing outfits with three-quarter-inch letters and a primer typewriter. They made alphabetical files of forty-eight-inch strips of oaktag with twenty-six pockets labeled with both small and capital letters. They prepared markers of oaktag with two sizes of perforations, a small one to let words show through and a long one for sentences.

The two teachers had the results of tests which had been made and therefore knew that the children had not learned to point to and name the alphabet letters. They decided to give the children as many as possible of the experiences which would lead to complete readiness.

The plan was consistently carried through until June. When school closed, half of the sixty children who were in attendance were well into the fourth stage, independent word recognition. Twenty were still in the third stage, transition from sight learning to independent word recognition. Ten were not ready for the second grade but they seemed to be overcoming the handicap of not having learned all of the alphabet letters and thus not having developed the essential automatic sound response to the "reliable" consonants.

The failure of the ten children, plus their partial success, is the reason for the stress which this report gives to the need for early mastery of the alphabet letters and the language sounds, and to the desirability of permitting those who learn quickly and easily to wait for those who seem to learn more slowly, a procedure which is used in the pages which follow.

In this report as it is written, what the children said is not included.

In practice, the teachers did not repeat what the children said in answering the questions. The form employed here is merely a device to avoid the dialogue form.

FIRST STAGE

Readiness

Step One

Objectives: To be sure that every child is learning the alphabet, is talking in sentences about the letters, and realizes that the teacher "reads" the names by looking at the words which are on the cards.

Materials needed: For each child, three cards with his name and one with the teacher's name; a box file for the teacher's desk; and a wall file with twenty-six pockets each labeled with a capital and a small letter.

Procedure:
We need to know each other's names. My name is Mrs. Reeder. I'll print it on the blackboard. I have a name card for each of you. Put it on your desk. Who knows the name of the letter at the beginning of *Mrs.?*

Yes, the first letter is *M.* Who knows the first letter of *Reeder?*

Yes, the first letter of *Reeder* is *R.* Let's all say my name.

I need to know your names, too. I have them here on these cards. This card has *Mary* printed on it. Mary, please come for your name card.

Here are two more name cards for each of you. Bring the one you have and find two others. Let's fasten one of them to the corner of your desk and put the others in this alphabetical file. Let's begin with the first letter.

Look at your names. If the first letter is *A*, bring the cards and put them in the *a*-pocket.

Bring your name cards and we'll put them at the letter where they belong.

Get one of your name cards from the alphabetical file. I need one of your cards in my little box file. Watch while I make a record of your work today.

In a few days I'll know your names, but right now I have to read them from your name cards. While we are walking over to the store, I'll need to be sure about your names, so I'll fasten your cards to your clothes.

You'll need to get your name cards from the alphabetical file. When we come back to the classroom, you can put them in the file again.

Let's put the name cards in the file. While we are putting them where they belong, let's read the alphabet down from the *a* at the top to the *z* at the bottom. Who would like to point to the letters?

Milton, you point to a letter and say its name, then all of us will say it. You say, "This letter is . . ." and name the letter. Then we'll say, "That letter is . . ." and we'll say the name of the letter at which you pointed.

Soon, everyone will know all of the letters.

Comment: This technique of recording only what the teacher says seems to indicate the activity through which the objectives were achieved. It leaves much to the imagination—and to memory.

The activity was sandwiched between the usual school routine. More than one day was required because the preschool experience of the children had not covered all of the twenty-point readiness requirements. The teachers proceeded to furnish the essentials.

While the children were talking, the teachers listened and noted the inaccuracies in pronunciation and errors in language usage but made no corrections during the period of adjustment to classroom exercises.

The teachers used only the print *a*, *g*, and *q*, the forms that are printed in the texts, to avoid requiring the children to learn three forms of the letters.

The teachers encouraged the children to move about freely when there was no need for quiet behavior. However, all of them were required to listen when someone was talking. Everything in the classroom was to be in the proper place, including the contents of the wastebasket. Every child was expected to be obedient and to behave politely.

Because none of the children seemed to measure less than six and one-half years mentally, the teachers decided they would try to guide even those who were "mentally" youngest toward success in learning to read.

Step Two

Objectives: To be sure that *every* child realizes that words give meaning to the people who look to find the meaning, and that the alphabet letters are in the words.

Materials: A little STOP sign for each child; a grocery store; a "play" store, with boxes, cans, bottles, and the like; printed words.

Procedure:

We are going in automobiles to the store. The drivers of the automobiles will go in the store with us. While we are inside, you must stay with your driver. Get your name cards from the file to give to her.

What will she do when she wants to speak to one of you?
Yes, she'll look at the cards and read your name.

When you want to know about something, ask your driver to tell you.

She will tell you her name. Do you think you can remember her name?

Yes, if you say her name a few times, you can remember it. When will be a good time to say it?

Yes, when you give her your card. She will say, "Thank you." What will you say when she thanks you for giving her your card?

Yes, you'll say, "You are welcome," and you can say her name, the way you say, "You are welcome, Mrs. Reeder" when I thank you for something.

Over at the corner, there is a STOP sign. It is big. Watch me while I print a big STOP sign on the chalkboard. What will the drivers do when the cars are at the STOP sign?

Yes, they will wait, and look both ways to be sure nothing is in the way.

Each of the drivers has some money to spend at the store. Your driver may ask you to take something from the shelves and put it in her basket.

Let's talk about our trip to the store. Let's look at the things in our play store. How do you know that this is a milk carton?

Yes, this word tells us that this is a milk carton. What is the name of the first letter?

Who can tell us the other letters? Point to the letters when you do.

Here are some words which are like the words on the things in the play store. Find a word and we'll stand it up by the word which it is like.

What is this? Yes, it is a little STOP sign. Tell us where you have seen STOP signs. There is a little STOP sign here for each of you.

Let's play some games with the little STOP signs. Let's play "store."

Comment: Much of the talking was done by those children who had been printing their names at home or in kindergarten. They had been experiencing the satisfaction which results from success. The teachers hoped to make it possible for every member of the class to experience some degree of success. With this in mind, they had the children who were willing to talk go in pairs with less talkative children; and after one child had talked, the other was asked to tell what he wanted to say.

When they were playing "store," the less talkative traded places with the other member of the pair and asked and answered what they had just heard the other child say.

Games with the STOP signs furnished opportunity for talk. The talkers did most of the planning, but every child said what he wanted to do or be.

Thus it was possible for the teachers to help the timid children become less timid and the talkative to await their turn for speaking.

There were many opportunities for use of the terms of politeness which are essential to good behavior. Moreover, in the common terms (*please, thank you, you're welcome, good morning, good afternoon, good-bye, how are you, very well, Mrs.*) and each other's names, the children were making—or learning to make—nearly all of the vowel sounds, most of the consonants, and two of the four diphthongs (*i* and *u*).

Step Three

Objectives: To begin "group response" so that every child will be speaking when to do so is desirable; to hold the interest of the children who already know the alphabet while those who do not learn so quickly are becoming able to point to and name all of the letters.

Materials: Twenty-six small boxes, on each of which one of the twenty-six alphabet letters is printed in both upper and lower case; paper lined for printing; crayons, chalk, and pencils; many sizes and colors of the letters *o, c, s, v, w, x,* and *z.*

Procedure:

Boys and girls, I'll read from this book a rhyme about the moon when it is hanging up in the sky like a big white ball. The woman who wrote this rhyme said the big white ball made her think that it looked like a great white eye. Only it couldn't be a great white eye because it doesn't wink the way you and I can wink. It doesn't blink, the way you and I can blink. It doesn't even frown, the way you and I can frown. It just seems to be looking down. Before I read it again for you to say it with me a line at a time, I'll draw a big round circle on the chalkboard; and in the middle of the rhyme I'll stop while we talk about a new word.

> There's a big round moon
> Like a great white eye
> Hanging up there
> Like a treasure in the sky.

A treasure is something we like. This ring is one of my treasures. Say *treasure* with me. Treasure. Like a treasure in the sky. Let's go on now.

> It never winks;
> It never blinks;
> It doesn't even frown;
> It just looks down.

Watch what I'm doing. I'm cutting a big circle from this square of paper. Now I'll cut a small circle from inside the big circle. This big circle with its center cut out is one of the letters of the alphabet.

What is the name of the letter? I'll print a big *o* and right by it I'll print another that is just half as high. I'll call the higher letter a capital *o* and the smaller letter a small *o.* You can say "capital."

Over on that shelf there is a box with two *o*'s printed on it. Who can find it? All right! Let's have a game. When I finish talking you may pretend you are having a nap. One by one, I'll touch you, so you will know you are to find the *o*-box. Ready! Take a nap, and I'll begin to touch you.

On this table there are many alphabet letters. You may pick up two *o*'s, a capital and a small one. Bring them to me and you may paste them on a sheet of paper.

You may have a pencil or a crayon or chalk and make some *o*'s. Watch me make an *o*, then you do the way I do. I start at the top and move my hand toward the left then around to the right to finish a circle.

How can you tell a capital *o* from a small *o*?

Yes, a small *o* is only half as high as a capital *o*.

We have here a printing set. We also have a sheet of this red paper for each of you.

Milton, you may find the two *o*'s and print them on your sheet of paper. Print the capital first at the top in the middle, then the small *o* near the capital.

Milton, you may help me for a few minutes. Then some other pupil may help.

Here are folders for you to keep your *o*-sheet in. Your name is on your folder. Print your name at the bottom of your *o*-sheet.

Watch what I'm doing. I've made this big *o*. Now I'll cut this part away, and you can see another alphabet letter. What letter is it?

Yes, it is *c*. Gloria, please come and print two *c*'s, a capital and a small *c*.

Everyone may print *c*'s.

Get what you need.

As soon as you are printing good *c*'s, you may get a sheet of blue paper and make a *c*-sheet to put in your folder.

I'm going to print another capital and small letter. While I'm printing the letter, please be still. You may know what the letter is, but don't even whisper it. I'll stand over in the corner and you come one by one and whisper the name to me. Bring your name card when you come. I'll keep your card today, but you'll find it in the file tomorrow.

We are ready! Watch me print this letter. I'll begin at the top.

Come and whisper the name of the letter.

Print the *s* and make a page for it.

Four more letters are alike for the capitals and the small letters. Shall we make pages of the other four to keep in our folders?

While you are printing the other four letters, those of you who know all of them already may help the others learn them.

Shall we work hard until everyone knows every letter?

As soon as everyone knows every letter, we can begin to read.

Comment: With each child whispering the name of the letter, the teachers could know whether any of them had not learned. The value of this information cannot be overestimated. That this was true of the children in the two first grades was proved in February when all of them who knew the alphabet were reading at their grade level and those who were not doing so did not know all of the letters.

The teachers found that the children learned the *s* readily and made the *s*-pages for their folders. However, many of them pronounced the name (*ess*) as if it were spelled with *i* (*iss*). The teachers showed how to make the vowel sound correctly by opening the jaws wide enough to let the right sound come out. They had the children play games which required *yes*, and buy and sell things in the play store priced *ten cents*. They taught the verse about the moon-in-the-sky; for they knew it affords practice on all of the language sounds except the *sh* (*she, surely*) and the breathy *th* sound (*thin*).

The two teachers found that memorization of the verse did not eliminate inaccuracies from the children's talk. For example, those who said *eye* and *sky* in the verse did not make the sound of *i* in *five* or *I*. Instead they said the words with the sound of *a* that is in *all*. They eliminated the final consonant sound of many words. They made substitutions which are characteristic of infant speech (baby talk). One child said *big* in the verse but said *doe* instead of *go*. Several said *like* in the verse but *wike* or *yike* when talking.

After all of the children had made pages for the seven letters which are alike in both upper and lower case, they learned and made pages for the remaining letters in the following order:

The two (*K k* and *U u*) which are nearly alike but are actually four letters.

The four (*J j, P p, Q q,* and *Y y*) which are nearly alike but the small letters hang halfway down below the line and actually are eight letters.

The thirteen (*I i, L l, F f, E e, D d, B b, R r, H h, T t, N n, M m, G g,* and *A a*) which differ greatly and are actually twenty-six different letters to be learned.

While the children were learning both forms of the three letters (*l, m, n*) whose names require open jaws, the teachers gave additional talking experiences; and while they were learning the two forms of the letter *r*, the teachers showed how the tongue rises toward the top of the mouth instead of remaining at the bottom.

During the learning time, the children talked in pairs, one of the "quicker" being paired with one of those who required many repetitions. The fortunate "helpers" showed the slower children how to print with the strokes beginning at the right place and moving in the proper direction. The helpers helped but did not do the work.

SECOND STAGE

Memorized Reading

Step One

Objectives: To have the children memorize the sentence *What is your name?*; and to begin the development of the inner speech response to three letters (*h, w, and y*) which do not carry their sound in their name.

Materials: Strips printed with the question: *What is your name?*

Procedure:

I'm sure all of you can read your own name. I'll hold up a card with my name on it. One of you please come and tell us what the letters are.

Each of you go to the alphabetical file and get your name card, then tell us what the letters are. You will be spelling your name.

I have a sentence here. This sentence asks a question. One of you may hold the sentence strip for me to look at. I'll read it and say something which will let you know that I have read it.

When Jane held the sentence strip for me to read, I read it; then what did I say?

Yes, I said, "My name is Mrs. Reeder."

Look at the sentence. Here are four words. The four words say: "What is your name?"

I'll hold the sentence strip before some of you. If you remember what the question is, you answer it so that I'll know you have read it.

On the table there are some sentence strips. Bring one to me and tell me what it says. Whisper so only you and I can hear.

Each of you may have a strip on your desk. Let's hold one

before someone to find out whether he remembers what the question is.

Comment: The sight-meaning-speech associations begin to develop the first time the learner looks at the *wh* of *what*. Because the speaker makes the breathy *h* sound before he vocalizes the sound of *w*, the inner speech develops as *hw*. Because the four words (*is, my, name,* and *what*) are to be learned as units, the inner response to the four units will develop.

Step Two

Objectives: To have the children memorize and then read a sentence which will have the same words at the beginning but a different word at the end, thereby developing the left-to-right movement of the eye focus; and to make sure that every child has remembered the first sentence.

Materials: Strips with *My name is* and a blank space (_____).

Procedure:

Boys and girls, we are going to the library. We don't make any noise in a library. We speak very softly. You may look at all of the books and choose one to bring back to the classroom. The librarian will put a card in your book. Your name will be printed on the card. We'll keep your books on our library shelf, and you can take them to your chairs whenever you have time to read them.

Let's talk about our visit to the library. I think I've learned all of your names, but right now I'll read a name from my little box file. Elsie, please bring your book and tell us something about it.

Your books have pictures. They have words, too. Can you find some of the letters? Can you print some of the letters on some of the pages in your alphabet letter folder?

While you are busy with your library books, I'll call you to come one by one, to read for me. Felix, you come first.

Felix, do you remember what this sentence strip says?

That's right. It says, "What is your name?" What is the name on this card?

Yes, this is my name. I'll fasten my name at the end of this strip. I'll read this sentence to you. "My name is Mrs. Reeder."

Tell me the name of the letters in *Mrs. Reeder* and in your name. I'll fasten your name card at the end of one of these strips. When I ask you what your name is, you can read this sentence. Read it.

Yes, your sentence says, "My name is Felix." I'll hold the question sentence for you to read to me. Then I'll read my sentence to you. My sentence is, "My name is Mrs. Reeder."

I'll read the question sentence to you and then you read your sentence.

Yes, you read your sentence. Tell me again what your sentence says.

I'll keep your sentence here and give it to you later.

Sarah, please come to read to me.

Every one of you remembered the question sentence; and all of you have read the new sentence. In a moment, I'll hold one of the sentence strips where all of you can see it. I'll stand here. You come, too.

The tallest will stand at the back.

I'll turn the sentence strip so you can see what is on it. As soon as you know what it says, read it to me.

Now I'll show you one of the sentences again, and you read it to me.

Yes, I showed the same sentence. You read it, too. Good for you!

I'll show the other sentence, but I'll read it to you because you will see my name at the end. "My name is Mrs. Reeder."

I'll put one of your names at the end. If you know the name, hold up your hand; then those of you who know the name may read the sentence.

Here are sentence strips for all of you. Bring your cards from the alphabetical file and we'll clip them at the blank space.

You may read the sentence to me and to the class.

You may have both sentences and use them to ask each other the question. Read the question, then read the answer.

Comment: The library experience kept the children occupied while the teacher was working with them individually. In such individual teaching, the teacher was able to write on each card a reminder of the child's needs.

As a result of knowing the needs of each child, the teacher can help him make the important first steps so that he can have an even start on his road to reading success.

Up to this time the children have been practicing the first of two habits which are essential to reading success. They focused their eyes on words (STOP, their names, the teacher's name, and words on boxes and cans). If they were thinking the meaning, they were reading silently; and if they pronounced the word, inner speech was developing. The second habit is operating when the eye focus is passing along the line of words from the left to the right, the habit they were learning.

The children memorized the sentences as units of meaning. Children who already are reading—and some of those in this class probably were—may have learned the poor habit of keeping the eyes focused on the words while pronouncing them. If the eyes remain focused on the words during pronunciation, the inner speech response may become overdeveloped. It is when inner speech is overdeveloped—exaggerated—that people's lips move during reading. These children were not looking at the words while they were speaking.

The safe way to avoid the poor habit is to have the learner look at the word only long enough to think the meaning and pronounce it a few times while studying it, then look away. The looking away may be either to tell someone the meaning or to read silently along the line.

During this second step, the teachers asked the children to read to them or to each other. No child was asked to look at the sentences while he was telling the meaning.

Step Three

Objectives: To be sure that the eye focus is passing along the line from left to right; to develop the inner speech response to the *th* sound.

Materials: A sentence strip with *This is my name;* the alphabet folder.

Procedure:

On your desk are the two sentences you have learned to read. Pick up the sentence which asks a question about your name.

Thank you. Hiram, tell us what the other sentence will tell us.

I have another sentence for you. I've clipped my name at the end. All of you, come here where you can see this sentence and the chalkboard.

I have Milton's alphabet pages here. Milton, please get the page with *n*.

I have printed the two sentences here. Please look at the sentence at the top. What is the first word? What is the last word?

Who can find *name* in the second sentence?

I'll print *name* right under *name*. What letter shall I print first?

Yes, I'll print *n* first. Tell me the letters to print next (*n a m e*).

I'll print a small *m* under this capital *m*, and a small *y* under this *y*. Who can tell us what this word is? Yes, this word is *my*. What is this word (*is*)?

I'll tell you the first word while I'm printing it. I've printed *Th*. See what my tongue does when I look at *th*. My tongue comes between my teeth, just a little tiny bit of it. You let your tongues come a tiny bit between your teeth. You make that sound with me. We'll make the sound while we look at the *th*. Now I'll print the last part of the word. I'll print an *i* and an *s*. This word is *this*. Say the sentence with me while my chalk runs along the sentence. *This is my name.* I think, "This is my name" because my name is clipped at the end. You think your own name while you read.

Here are sentences for you.

Put this new sentence on your desk.

Look at the sentence and say, "This is my name." Now say with me, "I think my own name while I'm saying the sentence."

Put your *My-name-is* sentence on your desk.

I can see your two sentences while I'm walking up and down. I think I can read them, too. I'm sure I can read them if you hold them up so the print is standing up. Let's try.

Myrtle, hold up a sentence. Let's all of us look at it.

The sentence says, "What is your name?" Is that what it says, Myrtle?

Please turn the *What-is-your-name* sentence over so that we can see only the *This-is-my-name* sentence.

Let's all move about and find out whether everybody has the *This-is-my-name* sentence for us to see.

Get a piece of drawing paper and cover both of the sentences. Now pull one of them from under the paper and ask the pupil in the next seat to read it to you.

Cover all of both sentences except the first word. Ask your friend to tell which sentence is the *What-is-your-name* sentence.

Cover the sentences but leave the first word of one sentence uncovered. Ask someone to tell what the sentence is.

You may now look at your library books, or print or go in pairs and quietly read to each other. I'll be at my desk. When I call your name, come and read to me.

Comment: At the desk the teachers made a note on the card of each child who was still making the sound of the diphthong *i* (*my*) as if it were spelled with another letter, or the sound of *e* that is in the name of the letter *n* (*enn*) as if the *e* were using the sound of *i* that is in *it* and *in*. They hoped these children would learn new speech habits regardless of the speech environment in their homes.

When the teachers—and the learners—say the word *sound*, the children will understand that a sound is a noise, which a sound is.

The importance to the children of making many repetitions of the two *th* sounds cannot be overestimated. These two sounds (*this* and *think*) require the only tongue movement that is not made while the alphabet letters are being said *if the names of the letters are being pronounced correctly*. Both of the sounds require a thrust of the tongue between the teeth. The vocal cords are vibrating while one of the sounds is being produced (*this, breathe*) but are not vibrating for the other sound (*think, breath*). Whether the vocal cords are vibrating does not seem to be important, for in the English language the tendency is to say the word in the easiest way. (We have discarded the sound of the *i* in *business* and the latest dictionary has eliminated the first *r* of *February*.) What is important to the learning-to-read experience is for the learner's inner speech to produce one of the *th* sounds when the mind is trying to recognize an unknown word.

While the left-to-right movement of the eye focus along the line of print is becoming habitual, the teachers must be sure that the children look at the first word. This is being done when the children cover the last part of the sentences with a marker.

Success in learning the second essential habit, forward movement of the eye-mind activity, should result from the repetitions of the three sentences.

Children who learn rapidly and those who seem to be reading can help those who learn at a slower rate.

Step Four

Objectives: To have the children study the words which are in the sentences; to use the *This-is-the* sentence strip while talking about things that are in the classroom.

Materials: Printed words (*What, is, your, name, My, my, This, book*) and the sentence strip "*This is the* _____" for each child.

Procedure:

If you know what this (*What is your name?*) sentence says, please stand. Hold the sentence toward me and tell me what it says. Put it on your desk and come here.

I'll cut off the first word of this sentence (*What is your name?*). Hold your hand up if you know it.

Yes, Alice, the word is *what*. Please hold it.

I'll cut off the second little word. What is it? Philip, you hold this *is*.

I'll cut off the next word. What is it? James, you may hold *your*.

Hold up your hand if you *don't* know this last word.

What are the first two letters?

Watch while I print *na*. The *na* is *na* (*nay*), then I'll print *m*. Say *name* with me. I have to print an *e* at the end to make the word right.

You four people, put the words along the shelf to make the sentence.

Peter, mix them together. Who will try to make them into a sentence?

Here on the table are words enough for each of you to have four. Get four and take them to your seat. Put each word on the word which is like it.

Put your *My-name-is* sentence with your name card at the end on your desk. You can get the first word from this box of words which begin with *m*. You'll have to use two words from your other sentence. Make the words match.

Cover the words of the other sentence (*This is my name.*) with matching words. Look in the alphabet boxes for the words you don't have on your desk.

Come here and see what I'm going to do. You know this sentence. Read it.

I'll cover the last word with this book. What does the sentence tell?

Yes, the sentence tells that this is my book.

Here is a sentence for you. Watch while I put a word on the book. The word is *book*. Read your sentence.

Here is a sentence strip which is like the first part of your sentences which say "*This is my name*" and "*This is my book*." This one has another word after "*This is*." The little word is *the*. So all of you tell me what this sentence strip says. Yes, it says "*This is the*" and it has a blank space for you to put words. Cover the *This-is-the* over the first three words of your sentence about your book. Read the sentence you have now. (*This is the book.*)

Take your *This-is-the* sentences to the play store and talk about things in the store.

Talk about the furniture in the classroom.

Comment: In the procedures which were covered during the readiness stage of learning to read, every child was taught the alphabet, had printed the twenty-six letters in both capital and small form, and had experiences which developed skill in using the letters in sequence.

All of the children are able to understand that people find out something because they look at words. All of them have used specific letters in filing their names, and , in consequence, accept the fact that words are made up of alphabet letters. All seem able to focus their eyes on words.

Now that the procedures are dealing with the memorization stage, the children should be gaining a "sight" vocabulary, and their eyes should be working with their minds in the essential left-to-right progress along the line. With a fair number of repetitions, this should be accomplished; for the three sentences require the eye and the mind to begin at the first of the line of words and to finish at the end.

Every child should learn seven words (*is, My, my, name, This, What, your*); and the children who seem to be learning the most easily can no doubt make sentences using the second form of three words (*Is, Your,* and *this*), as: *Is this your name? Is this my name? Your name is* _____.

The teacher can be sure that every child is learning every word because she examines the work of every learner.

This quality of teaching requires undivided attention throughout all learning situations.

There can be no misbehavior. No teacher should have to cope with children who choose to caper or otherwise refuse to do what is expected of them. Such children should either be returned to the kindergarten or placed in an environment where they can be taught what they have not yet learned. They should not be permitted to handicap either the teacher, or the children who are ready for reading success.

In the activity with the *This-is-the* sentence, the children are being made "ready" for sight learning of words which name things in the classroom. They should *see the word and hear it pronounced while they are thinking its meaning,* so that the associations will begin to be made in the proper order, meaning-sight-pronunciation.

Conversation about a telephone will plant the meaning in the talking vocabulary of all of the children. When they see the phone and the word at the same instant, sight learning will be begun.

The short form of the word is used because the learner

should see *ph* at the beginning of a word and should develop its inner speech sound of *f* before he sees the *p* without the *h;* for in all other combinations, the *p* uses its alphabet sound.

Step Five

Objectives: To teach *phone* in the symbol-to-meaning way; to use *here* and *where* in talk.

Materials: A real or toy telephone; pictures of telephones for each child; words: *a, phone.*

Procedure:

Please come and get a picture of a phone.

Here is a real (a toy) phone. Watch what I'm going to do. I'm placing this word right on this phone. This word is *phone.* Here are enough words for each of you to have one. Place your word *phone* on your picture. Look at your word and say *phone, phone.* Take your picture and your word to your desk.

What are the first two letters? Yes, the first two letters are *p* and *h.*

Let's spell *phone.* We'll say the two first letters (*ph*), then the others.

Get your *This is the . . ."* sentence strips. Put *phone* at the blank space.

One by one, come to me and read the sentence.

Watch what I'm doing with this "This is the . . ." sentence strip. I'm placing a tiny little word over *the.* Now the sentence is "This is a phone."

Please come and get this little word and cover the *the.* Let's all read the new sentence.

Take the little *a*-word off and read the sentence with the *the.*

Let's play a hide-and-seek game. To play hide-and-seek, one of you goes out of the room. One of you hides something. Dorothy, you be the one who goes out of the room. Bernice, you hide something in somebody's desk. This big red pencil will be all right. When you come back in, Dorothy, you go from one of us to someone else and ask, "Where is the pencil?" No one will tell you until you ask the one who has it. When you find it, the one who has it is to say, "Here is a pencil."

Dorothy, choose someone to go out. Bernice, choose someone to hide the pencil.

Comment: There are many variations of the hide-and-seek game; but at this point the learners need to use the *Here-is-the* phrase in preparation for a checking device that will make it possible for the teacher to be certain that every child looks at the first word of the sentence and does not merely remember or else say what he has heard some other child say.

Caution: In speaking about the indefinite article (*a*), avoid speaking the name of the first alphabet letter (*a*). Children should pronounce the word correctly; and they will do so unless they are permitted to call it a letter instead of the word which it is. The three articles (*the, an, a*) seldom are in a position of emphasis. Usually they are within a phrase and, as such, are spoken much as if they are syllables of long words. Adults who give the sound of the alphabet name to the *a*-word are merely carrying on an incorrect habit which some teacher permitted them to learn.

Notice that the indefinite article is not listed as a word to be learned. The other indefinite article (*an*) will cause no trouble. The children will imitate the speech in their environment. If they hear *a apple,* they may have to be taught to say *an apple.* But when they read, they see *an* before a word which begins with a vowel sound and they read what they see.

Step Six

Objectives: To teach that "Here is a phone" means the same as "This is a phone"; to have many repetitions of the left-to-right eye movement.

Materials: The sentence strips; the word *window* printed on cards.

Procedure:

The first word on this sentence strip is *here*. What does the sentence say?

Who will clip a word on the blank space at the end?

Put the two sentences on your desk. You have only one picture of a phone. Put the picture at the end of the *This-is-a-phone* sentence. Let's read it. Put the picture at the end of the *Here-is-a-phone* sentence. Let's read it. Tell us whether the two sentences mean the same. Yes, they do mean the same.

What is the letter at the first of *here?* How many small *e*'s in *here?* Let's name the four letters in *here*. When we name the letters we are spelling.

Watch my tongue while I'm saying *here*. Can you see it going up? I can feel it going up to make the *r*-sound. Can you feel the tip of your tongue going up while you are saying *here?* Let's all say the word. Let's read the sentences.

Mary and Alice, take my sentences to the window. Mary, you show a *This-is-a-window* sentence for us to read. Alice, you show us a *Here-is-a-window* sentence for us to read. Do both of the sentences mean the same window?

Mary, you show one of the sentences for Alice to read. Then, Alice, you show one of them for Mary to read. We'll watch to be sure you read them well.

Go about the room reading sentences to each other. Read them to me, too.

Comment: In order to read correctly, the children must look at the first word and then at the last one. The eye focus will move along the line.

Each time a child reads aloud, he should glance at the text to be sure that he knows what he is to say. None should learn the habit of trying to remember or of guessing.

The left-to-right habit is the key to independent word recognition. The eyes move forward rapidly while inner speech is producing the sounds. The learners hear the needed word.

The sentences might be changed to "*The phone is here.*"

There should be talk about the small and the capital *h* at the beginning of *here*.

Step Seven

Objectives: To have the children add words to their sight vocabulary; to be certain that each learner sees the object and word with the two close together; to provide enough repetition for permanent learning; to have the children talk about the letters in the words; to require everyone to make the consonant sounds correctly; to prepare booklets.

Materials: Three sentences (*This is my book. My name is* _____. *This is my name:* _____), printed and typed (primer-size type); paper for "little" book covers; one word printed (*fork*).

Procedure:

Look at this sentence (*This is my name*). I'll cover the last word with my notebook. What does the sentence tell you now? Dick, tell us.

Yes, it tells us that the notebook is mine.

I'd like to hear all of you read a new sentence.

While I hear you read to me one at a time, you may do something you'd like to do. What would you like to do?

Yes, you may print. You know that you must talk as quietly as if you were in the library. Can more than two be printing at the same time? What will the others do while two are printing?

I'll call your name for you to come. After you've finished reading to me, you may go out to play. Soon, all of you will be out playing.

Alice, you may come first. We'll talk so softly that no one will hear us. Read this sentence (*This is my name*). I'll cover the last word with a new word. When I cover the last word of the sentence, you will see something we eat with and the new word (*fork*). Read the new sentence (*This is my fork.*).

Yes, the new word is *fork*. Tell me the name of the letters.

I have some sentences for you to read. They were typed so they would fit in a little book. We'll make some books for you to take home to let your family hear you read. Go in pairs and read to each other.

Come here to the chalkboard. Let's talk about this *book*-word. I'll print it very big. What kind of letter is the first one? Yes, it is a capital *b*.

What is the last letter? Yes, it is small *k*. Will someone put two capital *o*'s instead of these small *o*'s? With *B O O* we must have a capital *K*. Who will print a capital *k* at the end of the word?

Let's print *book* three ways (*book, Book, BOOK*).

All of us will say the word correctly. We'll make a good *k*-sound at the end. Let's all say what I just said, "Let's make a good *k*-sound at the end."

What shall we print on the outside of our books? Yes, we'll print *MY BOOK* on them.

Comment: The procedure covered the six objectives. Owing to the teacher's resolve to know whether each child was learning what she was trying to teach, the children focused their eyes on the word and the book at the same moment. They made several repetitions. They pronounced the word with its final sound (*k*) instead of the sound of *t* or silent. Each child read the typed sentences and took part in the preparations for the little books they would read to their family.

However, some of the children were not able to read without help. It was necessary to provide additional experience with the alphabet for those who had been absent during a part of the activity to develop readiness. The letters in the printing set furnished much additional experience. The children printed in pairs. The teachers could trust the "helper" to see to it that the letters were kept in alphabetical order. When a child needed a letter, he had to look for it, and after he had used it, he had to return it to its place. This experience with the sequence of the letters was profitable for both members of the team. It was an extension of the name-card filing and will be used in pasting words on the twenty-six pages on which they printed the fifty-two letters while they were learning the alphabet.

Step Eight

Objectives: To have the children read the three sentences and staple the sheets in the book covers; to have them alphabetize the sheets on which they printed the fifty-two letters; to have each child paste the words he knows where they belong in the alphabet "books."

Materials: A half-sheet of attractive construction paper for the cover; three sentences (*This is my book. My name is_____. This is my name _____.*) on three pages for the little books; the known words typed on oblongs of paper.

Procedure:
I have made a little book with sentences you have been reading. On the cover I've printed the name of my book. Inside, a sentence is on each page. How would you like to make a book like mine?

Yes, you may take it home and read it to your family.

This is the name of my book (*MY BOOK*). What is this word (*BOOK*)?

Yes, you printed it yesterday. I'll print the other word (*MY*) and two words right under it. If you know them, keep very still. Don't even whisper. I'll go to my desk and you come one by one and speak softly while you tell me the words.

Here is paper for your book covers. Fold your cover the way mine is folded. Make the corners fit exactly right. What does *exactly* mean?

While two of you are printing, the others may do whatever you'd like to do. But we'll be quiet, of course.

Come here and look at the file where I keep the words you know. My sheets are like the sheets you have in your folders. Mine have the *a*-sheet at the first, just like our wall file.

I'll open my pages to the *m*-sheet. If you know the words, hold up your hand to let me know that you know them; but don't make a sound. I'll ask one of you to tell us. Tom, you tell us the words.

Larry, find the *w*-sheet. Where is *w* on our wall file? Yes, at the bottom.

Let's put your sheets in alphabetical order, from *a* to *z*. Find your *a-sheet*. It is the last sheet you made. Hold it where I can see it.

I'll show you how to make your alphabetical file the way I made mine.

Open your folder and put the *a*-sheet with its two *a*'s turned so we can't see the letters. You helpers on the back row, please look at the sheets on your row to be sure they are turned like mine is.

What letter shall we have next? That's right. Helpers, find your *b*-sheet and help me be sure all of the *b*-sheets are lying the right way.

What letter belongs next? [On to *z*.]

The words you have been reading in your sentences are on the shelf in the alphabet boxes. You may put the words you know on the pages where they belong. Be careful! You must keep the sheets in alphabetical order.

Comment: The children should read from their books to each other and to occasional visitors. They should bring the books back from home and should file them on a shelf or in a box where they can get them easily when a need arises. The alphabet folders should be kept where parents can see them. One solution would be to have a box for each child.

The little books will be more interesting if other pages are added, or if the children bring pictures or make drawings to show the meaning.

The alphabetical folders will be increasingly valuable as the "sight" words become more numerous. It is to be expected that capacity to retain sight words will vary from individual to individual. The children who seem to learn quickly usually can carry a heavier load of sight words than is retained by those who seem to learn more slowly. However, the learners who have the largest vocabulary may be entering the transition stage and are already on the way to independent recognition. Knowledge of the alphabet is an important factor. Accurate retention of rhymes is another.

Step Nine

Objectives: To add sight words; to put pages in the little books; to teach *"What is this?"*; to have the children name the letters in words.

Materials: Sentence strip (*What is this?*); typed sentences on pages for the little books (*This is a pencil. This is a fork.*); word: (*pencil*).

Procedure:

I have a sentence strip here. It has three words. It asks a question. The question asks to be told something. The first two words are the same as the first two words of this sentence (*What is your name?*) So the first part of the sentence is *What is?*

Now I'll print the last word. I'll print the last word under a word which you know because it is the first word of the sentence "This is my name."

Look at *This*. What kind of letter *t* is at the beginning of *this?*

Yes, it is capital *t*. I'll print a small *t* under the capital *t;* then three more letters under the three other letters of *This*.

What do you think the word is? Mary, tell us what you think the word is.

Yes, Mary, it is *this*. Read the sentence, Mary. Let's all read it.

I'll get something from the play store and hold up the question for you to read it. All of you answer the question by telling me what I'm getting.

One at a time, come to me to read. I'll give you something and a new word.

Yes, the word is *pencil*. Name the letters. What is the first letter? When you say the names of the letters you are helping yourself learn to read.

What is the letter at the end? I'd like you to say, "The letter at the end of *pencil* is *l*.

You said *pencil* exactly as I said it. You can say *end* the way I say it. Open your mouth a little wider and say *end*. You may take the word and the pencil to your desk.

Do you see the *c* in the middle of *pencil*?

What other letters do you see?

Now that all of you have read the question and have been printing your new word, let's talk about the colors of crayons and pencils. Let's talk about the colors of the pages in your alphabet folder.

Let's talk about the things in the play store.

Go in pairs and take turns reading the question while you touch something. Then listen while your partner tells the name of what you touch.

If I have a page for your little book that says, *"This is a pencil,"* do you think you can draw a pencil right by the word?

Comment: Each word should become organized into the reading vocabulary before another is presented.

As you were reading the procedure, you may have questioned the necessity for the teacher to spend so much time with each child. Your question may be answered by the voice of experience: in general, children who are successful during their first year continue to be successful and, conversely, children who fail continue to fail. They are stamped—or, what is worse, they stamp themselves—with the negative attitude which accompanies failure. There is no waste of time if a child is being guided toward a good start.

Step Ten

Objectives: To have the inner sound response developed to the two letters which spell the *sh* sound (*she, shoe, wish*) before the learners are expected to see the *s* without the *h;* to continue memorization of sentences which have the same words at the beginning but different words at the end; to have the children see the words for colors while they are seeing the colored paper.

Materials: Sentence strips (*Where is* _____? *She is here. Is she here?*); for each child, a set of colored—and black and white—paper cut in circles, squares, and rectangles; words: *where, she, She, Is, blue, yellow, red, green, orange, brown, purple, pink, black, white.*

Procedure:

Here is a new word (*where*). This sentence strip says "*Where is* _____?" I'll clip Alice's name on it. Jack, read the question. All read it.

Look at the first word. Come here where you can see what I'm going to do. I'm covering the *Where* with my marker. I'm moving the marker toward the right so that only the first two letters show. Everybody, say the two letters together the way I'll say them (*wh*). That's right. Let's say them again.

I'll tell you something about these two letters. Whenever you see them together like this, you can easily find out what the word is. You can help yourselves remember the words that you've learned in some other sentence. Let's look at the first two letters of *what*. Say *what*. Say *where*. Watch me while I say *where*. Let's say *while*. Let's say *when*.

I open my mouth when I start to say *what* or *where* or *when* or *while* or *white,* and some breath comes out. Let's say those words again.

Watch what happens right after the breath comes out. My lips are closing: *wh.* Let's all make that funny noise: *wh, wh, wh.* Let's turn that noise into *what.* Let's all watch ourselves to know what we're doing when we say *what* and *where.*

While my lips are closing, I can hear myself making another noise. When we say Walter's name, we make the same noise. When we say *we,* we make the same sound.

Let's look at the two letters again. I'll say "sound" instead of "noise." You say *sound* with me. Say this: "*A sound is a noise.*"

I'll clip Mary's name on this *Where-is* card. Who will read it?

That's right, John. I'll answer the question: *She is here.* This first word is *she.*

Mary, get the name of a girl from the file. We'll fasten the name on the *Where-is* sentence strip. Read the question, Mary. Who will answer the question by reading the sentence?

Two of you bring the question and the answer sentences up here to let us see you read to each other, and to us, of course.

Before you begin to read to us, glance at your sentence to be sure that you will say the right words. Then look up and read to your partner and us.

Barbara and Alice, you come to the front of the class and show us.

Look at the new word (*she*). What are the names of the first and second letters? Yes, the two letters are *s* and *h.* When we see the two letters together as they are in *she,* we can make the noise, the sound, which we can hear when we begin to say *she.* Let's say *she,* slowly, *she.*

Here is a sentence which answers the question "*Where is she?*" This sentence says, "*She is here.*"

Take the two sentences (*Where is Mary? She is here.*). Go in pairs and read to each other. Take turns reading questions and answers.

Here is the new word (*she*). Take two, one with a capital *s* and one with a small *s*. There is another word here for you. The *is*-word you have begins with a small *i*. This new word (*Is*) begins with a capital letter.

Can you read this question (*Is she here?*)? Come to my desk and read it to me in a whisper for just you and me to hear. I'll read the answer after you read the question.

Go in pairs to read to each other.

Some pieces of paper are on your desks. I need to know whether you know all of the colors. Hold up the red paper. Put it at the right-hand corner of your desk. Hold up the blue paper. Put it next to the red paper. [Ditto for the other eight papers provided.]

Here are the words which name the colors. There are ten of them, one for each piece of paper. Maybe you know some of the words. Put the word you know on top of the paper. Leave the words you don't know on the left-hand corner of your desk.

You are going out to play. Leave your papers and words where they are. I'll gather them and put them away.

Comment: By examining the papers and words, the teachers can know what to do about teaching the words. Children who already know them can be leaders in games which will provide enough repetition for every child to know all of them.

The children should see these words in print and use them in talk. They can do both in "races" where they try to see how quickly they can match the words to the colors. While playing games, they can use the letters as clues to aid in memorization. They can place together the words which begin alike (*blue, brown, black; blue, black; purple, pink*); words which have the letter *r* (*red, green, orange, brown, purple*); words which have the sound of *e* in *letter* (*red, yellow*); and so on.

Moreover, they can talk about the color of the things they see, such as the orange color of paper and an orange, the likeness in color of the yellow and the orange pencils, the many shades of red in apples; the pink shades that are so nearly like the reds; the many shades of purple; and so on.

Furthermore, this talk and the games furnish a learning situation for *orange* to be taught as a sight word.

The talk about the sounds of *th, wh,* and *sh* should result in some degree of understanding of the concept of sounds, so that talk may be begun about the sounds in words. Talk about the sounds which we hear in the words we read will expand to include talk about the sounds which the letters represent. Such talk—and the understanding which must be included—marks the beginning of the third stage, transition from memorized reading to independent word recognition. Children who have reached this stage but are kept waiting for the slower learners are not being penalized. Quite the contrary: by helping others they are becoming stronger.

Step Eleven

Objectives: To show the children how to use the letters as clues to aid in memorization; to increase the sight vocabulary; to talk about the sound of some of the letters.

Materials: Sentence strips reading "*In our play store we have_____*"; things in the play store; words (*milk, forks*) printed and typed.

Procedure:
Let's show our little books to our visitor. She will ask some of you to read to her. Show her your alphabet pages, those which have words on them.

Here is another sentence for you to learn. Come here where I am.

The sentence says, "*In our play store we have a fork.*"

Yes, Marvin, we do have more than one fork. We have many forks. We'll make the sentence say that we have forks in our play store. Marvin, take the last two words off. You can see that they are just clipped on. Horace, please get an *s* from the printing set. Print an *s* at the end of *fork*. The *s* makes the word say *forks*. Can you hear the sound of *s*?

Let's say the sentence word by word. (*In our play store we have forks.*)

Bernice, take this chalk and print a word while we tell you its letters. [All of the words printed by different children.]

Let's say the sentence while we look at the words. Let's say it again.

Here are your sentence strips, and two words (*forks, milk*). You may put them on your desks. Show *forks* to me. Put *forks* at the end of the sentence. Let's see whether you can remember what the sentence says.

Joe, stand up and tell us.

Mary, tell us we have bottles in our play store.

Gloria, tell us we have boxes. Ann, tell us we have milk in our store.

Show me the other word you took to your desk (*milk*). What is the name of the first letter? (The last letter? The letter just before the *k*?)

Hold up your hand if you know what the word is. Come here and whisper the word to me. When you go back to your chair, don't even whisper the word.

I'll print the word in big letters. How many letters are there in the word? Yes, you can count the letters. Each of the letters has a sound. I'll look at the *m* and make the sound of *m*. *M*. Watch how I keep my lips closed while I make the sound of *m*. Let's all make the sound. I'll move the chalk from the *m* to the *i* while I say the first part of the word (*mi*), then, while I move the chalk along, I'll let my tongue go up to make the next sound (*l*). You'll hear the *mil* of the word. When the chalk moves under the *k*, what sound will you hear?

Some of you made the sound of *k*. Hold up your hand if you know the word.

Let's make the sounds while the chalk moves along the word. Let's say *milk*.

Milton, what letter does your name begin with? Yes, Mary, your name does, too. What about the *Mrs.* in my name?

Get your alphabet folders and open them to *m*. Let's read the words. How many words do you have on your *m*-page? You may put your words on your pages. Where will you put *forks*?

Would you like to put the words about our play store in your books?

Turn to the page for the letter *i*. You have *is* with a small letter. Do you have it (*is*) with a capital letter? Here is *Is* for you to put in.

Let's read the sentences (*Where is* _____? *She is here. Is she here?*) which are on your desks. Why do you have a girl's name in the blank space?

Yes, you must have a girl's name when you say *she*.

When we ask the question which begins with *is* (*Is she here?*), we need another word in the answer. What word do we need? I said the word.

Yes, Walter, I said *yes*. Here it (*yes*) is on the board. What is the first letter? The last? Let me see the words on your *y*-page.

Let's have a boy's name in the *Where-is* question. With Jack's name in the question, what will we answer?

Yes, we'll answer, "*He is here.*" The other question (*Is she here?*) will have to be "*Is he here?*"

Shall we have the new word (*he*) here for you to put in your alphabet book?

Comment: Every learner who has mastered the left-to-right eye-mind habit and can hear and imitate the language sounds is well on the way toward independent word recognition. The teachers who have been taking children through the steps outlined and suggested here should continue the individual checking. They should also add words to the sight vocabulary but make sure that the children talk about the letters which are used in the words.

Talk about words and sounds is profitable provided no sound is made incorrectly and no child keeps his eyes focused on the words he is saying while he is reading aloud.

While the children are still in the memorization stage, they should learn to say many verses of the Mother Goose type. The two which have been used in the third step of the first stage (readiness) and in the first step of the second stage (memorization), use nearly all of the forty sounds that occur in the words of the English language. The sounds which are missing from the two, are in the verses which follow.

A happy little fairy
Went dancing on her way.
"Good morning!" she said to everyone,
"How do you do today?"

This happy little fairy
Came singing from her play.
"Good evening," she said to everyone.
"It's been a glorious day."

Ding-dong, ding-dong, ding-dong, ding-dong.
Ding-dong, ding-dong, ding-dong, ding-dong.
Hush! Hush! Hush! Hush! Listen to the bells.
Listen to the bells.
The big church bells, ding-dong, ding-dong.
The tiny toy bells, ting-aling-aling, ting-aling-aling.
Let the big bells ring, dong-ding, dong-ding.
Let the toy bells sing, ling-aling-aling.
Hush! Hush! Hush! Hush! Listen to the bells.
Ding-dong, ding-dong, ding-dong, ding-dong,
Ding-dong, ding-dong, ding-dong, ding-dong.

THIRD STAGE

Transition From Memorized Sight Learning
to Independent Word Recognition

Step One

Objectives: To have children continue to be thinking the exact meaning of the new words—and phrases—at the time they see, hear, and pronounce them; to add words and sentences to the books which have been started; to continue talking about the letters; to continue making the language sounds correctly; to do all reading silently before reading aloud.

Materials: The play store sentence typed on a page to be added to the little books, with *In our playstore* on one line and *we have* _____ on the line below, with an indentation as in real books; typed words ready for the alphabet folders.

Procedure:

Here is a page for your little books. Come to my desk to read it to me. After you read it, you may put it in your book. While one of you is reading at my desk, the rest of you may play store. Milton, you be the leader to hold this sentence (*In our play store we have* _____) where everyone can see it while telling what we have in our play store. I'll call your name when you are to read to me. After you read, you may go outside to play.

Here are words for you to put in your alphabet folders. Come and look at my alphabet folder. I've printed a title on mine. Who can read it? (*This Is My Word Book.*) Would you like to print a title on your folders? Before you go in pairs to print, let's make the sounds of the words. I'll print them on the board. Make the sound of each letter while I'm keeping my finger under it.

Look at each word in the title of our word books. What kind of letter is at the beginning of each word? Each word begins with a capital letter because *"This Is My Word Book"* is the name of my book. I could have had all of the words in capitals. Yes, you may have yours either way.

Shall we say the verse about the moon? Who will be the leader?

I'll read another verse. This verse says that our mouths are like a room and our tongues are like a broom. We can open the door wide. See how wide I open my mouth! We can sweep the walls. Can you move your tongue against your cheeks, inside? We'll sweep the floor. That isn't easy for me to do. I'll sweep the ceiling. I can put my tongue up in the top of my mouth. "Then," this verse says, "our tongues will be like good brooms," first-class, the verse says. And our mouths will be like well-cleaned rooms.

Would you like to say it with me?

I'll read a line, then we'll all say it. [So on for the verse.]

> My mouth is like a room.
> My tongue is like a broom.
> I'll play this game with you:
> We'll open wide the door;
> We'll sweep the walls,
> We'll sweep the floor;
> We'll sweep the ceiling too.
> Then our tongues will be
> Like first-class brooms;
> Our mouths will be
> Like well-cleaned rooms.

Comment: This verse affords practice for loosening the speaking muscles; but its value will be felt if the children put correct sound production in their conversation. The words use more than half of the vowel sounds, three diphthongs (*i*, *u*, and *ou-ow*), and all but six of the consonants.

The rather long list of objectives are all covered in the procedure.

Step Two

Objectives: To have the children dictate sentences which will be stories for their little books; to guide the children toward using words with letters which have not been used in other sentences.

Materials: Sentences and words typed for the books; such words as these: *big, boys, cars, cat, dog, five, for, four, girls, go, like, little men, one, saw, six, three, to, two, walk, we, went, women;* such sentences as:

> We went for a walk.
> We saw one little dog.
> We saw one big cat.
> We saw two men.
> We saw three women.
> We saw four little girls.
> We saw five little boys.
> We saw six big cars.
> We like to go for a walk.

Procedure:

Shall we go for a walk this morning? All right, let's line up by two's. When we are out on the pavement, let's walk with three in each row.

While we are out, shall we count the cars that we see?

Yes, we may as well count the people who are in the cars.

Yes, indeed, let's count the children and the cats and the dogs.

We had a good time, didn't we?

Let's make a page for our books. You tell me what to write.

What shall we say first? I'll print what Henry said (*We went for a walk.*). What did we see?

Comment: The twenty-three words in the sentences use three letters to which the automatic sound response—inner speech—was not developed either in the alphabet during the "readiness" stage or in the sentences which have been used in the memorization stage. The letters are *c*, *g* and *x*. The learners will see, hear, and speak the *k* sound of *c* and the *go* sound of *g* much more frequently than they will use the alphabet sound of each of the two letters.

The children will suggest sentences which use the letters.

They will read from their little books enthusiastically for every occasion. However, they must *always* glance at the text to read silently—and rapidly—before reading aloud. This habit is the basis of efficient reading.

The children should talk about the letters, but only sparingly about the sounds, because of the difficulty encountered when pronunciation of an isolated consonant sound is attempted. A consonant is being produced incorrectly when the least bit of vowel sound is included. The sound of *b* or *r* cannot be spelled with *buh* or *er*. The safe way to speak of a consonant sound is "the sound of *b*" or "the *k* sound of *c*" and "The *m* in *Mary* sounds exactly like the *m* in *Melvin*."

Step Three

Objectives: To furnish experience which will be pleasurable to the children while they learn words with letters not used in earlier sentences; to continue all good habits and avoid all that are detrimental.

Materials: Words typed for the books: *at, bear, can, chair, desk, just, jump, lion, me, not, read, school, see, sing, sit, will, work, words, write;* and such sentences as:

We can go to the zoo.
At the zoo we can see a big bear.
At the zoo we can see a lion.
A lion is just a big cat.
The lion will not jump at me.

I like to go to school.
I like to work at my desk.
I like to sit in my chair.
At school we read our books.
At school we write.
I can write words.
I like to write words.

Procedure:

We are going to the zoo tomorrow. Here are pictures of what we can see at the zoo. We have some books with pictures of what we can see.

I have some sentences about zoo animals. I'd better not give them to you now, though, because there are some words you may not know. However, I'll leave them on the library table. If anyone finds a sentence he would like to read, just bring it to me. I'll tell you the words you don't know.

Here is a sentence about school. (*I like to go to school.*) I'll print it on the chalkboard. What is this letter? Yes, it is capital *I*. When capital *I* is alone like this in a sentence, *I* is a word.

The second word is *like*. Who will point to the first letter and tell us what it is? Can you see a small *k* in the word? Who will point to it?

Look along the sentence. There are three tiny words. Who will tell us the words? Yes, the words are *to go to.*

Let's read as much as we can: "*I like to go to*" and the last word is *school.* Let's read the whole sentence. Who will read it? Who else?

Let's read the sentence again while I move the chalk underneath the words.

Look at the *ch* in *school.* In this word the *ch* has the sound of *k.* We say *skool.*

Comment: The teacher's hand will move smoothly forward at the rate of talk. The children's hands will do the same. Should there be any hesitation, the teacher can assist. This kind of exercise will guide the children's eyes. It will eventually lead them into seeing words which are farther along the line than the words they are speaking. This reading ahead with the eyes and the mind while the voice is talking is a skill which is practiced by every effective oral reader.

If every sentence is taught in much the same way that the first was dealt with, the children will remember most of the words, for every time a learner focuses his eyes on a word while he is pronouncing it, the eye-speech associations are being strengthened. Given enough repetition, the subsequent focusing of the eyes will produce the word in inner speech. The meaning associations are included provided the learner is thinking the meaning while he is pronouncing the words.

Step Four

Objectives: To teach *enough*; to continue talking about the letters in words; to learn some of the words which are on the boxes and cans in the "store."

Materials: The word *enough* on a card; things in the play store.

Procedure:

Do you know how many knives and forks and spoons we have in our play store? Yes, we can count them to find out whether we have enough for all of us.

I've printed parts of some long sentences on the board, but the last part of the sentences is covered by this paper. Who will read the part which is at the top?

Let's all read the part which is not covered. Before we begin to read aloud, let's all read as far as my chalk goes before we begin to speak.

We'll read *"In our play store"*; then we'll read it aloud. We'll read *"we have"* and I'll uncover the next word of the sentence, *"forks."*

I'll erase *forks* and print a new word after *"we have,"* and when I take away this other sheet of paper you can see more words. The last words will say *"for all of us."* Read them with me: *"for all of us."*

Let's read the long, long sentence while I move the chalk to keep ahead of us so everyone will know what to say.

> *In our play store*
>   *we have* (Here's the new word. It is *enough.*) *enough forks*
>   *for all of us.*

Let's look at the new word (*enough*). What is the first letter? What is the second letter? Yes, the letter *e* sounds exactly like the *e* in the alphabet. Take a card which has *enough* printed on it. Let's say some sentences which have the new word in them. What is your sentence, Melvin?

I'll uncover all of the long sentence. Let's read it.

> *In our play store*
>   *we have enough spoons*
>   *for all of us.*

Comment: Children should see *enough* in meaningful situations enough times to develop an automatic sound response to the word. Later, their inner speech will produce the correct pronunciation of words which rhyme (*rough, cough,* and the like) *when the words are seen in a meaningful situation.* They should not be told that *ough* uses the sound of *f,* because of other words (*through, though, thought*). Inner speech ignores silent letters as they are ignored in vocal speech.

Even though children talk about the letters and the sounds of words, they soon see the words as units *provided they have learned to look along rapidly from left to right.* Word-by-word reading should never be learned.

Step Five

Objective: To show that naming the letters in a word is spelling.

Procedure:

Let's look at this word (*here*). When you print it with the printing set, how do you know which letters to get? In which part of the line of letters will you find the *h*? The *e*? The *r*?

Who will go to the alphabetical file and point to the letters while we say them? Who will point to the letters while all of us say the letters in the word where it is printed on the board?

Who will say the names of the letters without looking at the word?

Let's pretend we are printing it in front of us. Let's pretend we are beginning it with a capital letter.

Open your alphabet books at the right place for the word. If you don't have *here* on your page (for *h*), you may take two typed words from the alphabet boxes and paste them where they belong. Why do you need two words?

Yes, you need one with a small letter and one with a capital letter.

I'll print this word (*spoon*) on the chalkboard. Let's learn to spell it. I'll pronounce it, then while I draw the chalk under the letters, we'll say them, and then we'll pronounce the word again. We are learning to spell the word this way. Who will move the chalk under the word while we spell it?

Let's make a list of the words we have learned to spell. Let's make books for our spelling words. How many pages do you need?

You write the words while I pronounce them for you.

Comment: One of the outcomes from spelling is the additional repetitions for the children who seem to learn less quickly than others.

In learning to spell, the children are taking the first steps leading to permanent skill in spelling this difficult-to-spell English language. The first spelling words should use letters which are dependable in the sense that when the sound is heard, the letters will occur in the word. The dependables are *b, d, h, l, m, n, p, r, y, w, wh, th, sh* at the end of words, and *v* except in one word (*of*). Most consonant blends are dependable in spelling.

FOURTH STAGE

Independent Word Recognition

Objective: To be sure that each child is sounding rapidly from left to right through the words that occur in his reading material; to be sure that each child has developed—or is developing—the sounds of all of the consonant letters and combinations of letters; to be sure that each child is making all of the consonant sounds correctly and is making the vowel sounds with the jaws far enough apart for good pronunciation; to have the children become able to place words in lists according to initial consonants, final consonants, consonant blends, silent letters, vowel sounds, and so on.

Materials: Either blackboard space to preserve lists of words or cards of printed words.

Procedure:

Let's put the words we are learning in the lists where they belong.

Yes, *table* belongs with words which begin with *t*. Where else?

Yes, it belongs with words which end in *ble*. Where else?

Yes, it belongs with words in which the *a* uses the sound of *a* in *make*.

When you see a word you don't know, ask me to help you. The vowel letters have so many different sounds that you may need to be told which sound is in the word.

Comment: When one of the less common consonants occurs in a word, tell the children about it. In order to be sure of permanency, put other sentences on the board to furnish additional repetitions and make duplicate copies on the primer typewriter for the children to put in their booklets.

Remedial Reading at the First Level

Non-readers who have had a year in the first grade without having learned to read should be taken through the four stages which are essential to beginners: readiness, memorization, transition from memorization (sight learning) to independent word recognition, and independent word recognition.

They may be taken through the first stage rapidly because they are likely to know some of the alphabet letters and their eye focus may be moving along the line from left to right. However, *every pupil should know every letter in both upper and lower case.* An excellent device for review or for initial learning is to print and name the seven letters which are alike in both upper and lower case (*Oo, Cc, Ss, Vv, Ww, Xx, Zz*), then two others which are nearly alike (*Kk, Uu*), and four which extend below the line (*Jj, Pp, Yy, Qq*), and the other thirteen in about the following order: *Ii, Ll, Ff, Ee, Dd, Bb, Rr, Hh, Tt, Nn, Mm, Gg, Aa.* Beginners should not be required to learn the manuscript writing form of three letters—a, g, and q—until they are learning to write. No data are available to show how many children have failed to learn to read because they were puzzled by having to see the manuscript writing a and g instead of the print forms.

Beginners who can name the alphabet letters can use them as memory clues while they are gaining the first vocabulary, an essential of the second stage. With this definite knowledge of the letters and continual use of the letters, the learners are likely to begin using the sounds of the letters. Use of the sounds in connection with the left-to-right movement of the eye focus along the line means that the learners are in the third stage because they are making the transition from the sight learning to independent word recognition, the fourth stage.

By the time the fourth stage is reached, the pupils have developed the inner sound response to all of the consonant letters which spell single sounds, to the combinations of letters which spell the two-letter sounds, and to the consonant blends. Moreover, they have developed the inner speech response to hundreds of words as units, so that the eye focus passes so rapidly across the words that the speech muscles do not articulate the sounds and there is no word-by-word reading nor evidence of lip movement during silent reading. Furthermore, they have no difficulty with silent letters; and if the word they hear in their inner speech does not fit into the meaning of the sentence, they ask for help.

By the time adult beginners have reached the fourth stage, they will have remembered what they have been told about the sounds of the vowel letters and will be becoming able to secure help from a dictionary.

Beginners who can name the alphabet letters and have developed the left-to-right eye habit should be taught the three sounds which do not carry their sound in their name, the *h,* the *w,* and the *y.* The three may be learned in the sentence: What is your name? The sound of *h* is produced before the sound of *w* (*hwat*). The inner sound response will develop to both *h* and *w.*

The learners should see words with *th, sh,* and *ph* before they learn words which begin with *t* or *s* or *p.* The *ch* sound should be avoided until after the pupils learn *school* as a sight word. Because *can* and *go* are needed, the two words should be taught as sight words. The *n* of *name* is always the sound of *n* at the beginning of words and at the end, so that beginners can talk about both the name and the sound of the two consonant letters.

The alphabet for non-readers at the beginning level

Beginners of all ages who can point to and name the alphabet letters are already well on the way toward learning to read, for they—without being conscious of what has been happening—have already developed the marvelous inner sound response (inner speech, phonics) to one sound of each of twenty-three of the letters. This is good, as far as it goes, but it leaves much to be done about the five vowels and some of the others.

The following charts present a scheme that shows relative values of the letters.

25 CONSONANT SOUNDS SPELLED BY 21 LETTERS

SPELLED BY ONE LETTER	DUPLI-CATED	SPELLED BY TWO LETTERS	NOT SPELLED BY ANY LETTER
b	ph (f)	ch (k, sh)	g as in go
d		ph (f)	
f		sh (s without h)	
h		th (this)	
j		th (three)	
k		wh (hw)	
l		zh (s or z, never zh)	
m		ng (n in ink, finger)	
n		8	
p	(Omit	− 1	
r	ph as f:)	7	
s			
t		1 (add g)	
v			
w			
y			
z			
17		17	
		25 consonant sounds	

26 LETTERS TO SPELL 40 SOUNDS

One sound in each			SOUND MISSING FROM NAME
VOWEL	DIPH-THONG	CONSO-NANT	
a		*b*	
		c (*s*)	
		d	
e		*f*	
		g (*j*)	*h*
	i	*j*	
		k	
		l	
		m	
		n	
o		*p*	
		q (*k*)	
		r	
		s	
		t	
	u	*v*	*w*
		x	*y*
		z	

18	3
3	
21 consonants	
5 vowels	
26	
− 3 (*h, w, y*)	
23 to which inner speech has been developed	
3 to which the inner response should be developed	

INDEX